D0224944

THE WORKINGS OF OLD TESTAMENT NARRATIVE

THE SOCIETY OF BIBLICAL LITERATURE
SEMEIA STUDIES
Dan O. Via, Jr., Editor
William A. Beardslee, Associate Editor

THE SWORD OF HIS MOUTH: FORCEFUL AND
IMAGINATIVE LANGUAGE IN SYNOPTIC SAYINGS
  by Robert C. Tannehill
JESUS AS PRECURSOR
  by Robert W. Funk
STUDIES IN THE STRUCTURE OF HEBREW NARRATIVE
  by Robert C. Culley
STRUCTURAL ANALYSIS OF NARRATIVE
  by Jean Calloud, translated by Daniel Patte
BIBLICAL STRUCTURALISM: METHOD AND
SUBJECTIVITY IN THE STUDY OF ANCIENT TEXTS
  by Robert M. Polzin
STORY, SIGN, AND SELF: PHENOMENOLOGY AND
STRUCTURALISM AS LITERARY–CRITICAL METHODS
  by Robert Detweiler
CHRISTOLOGY BEYOND DOGMA: MATTHEW'S CHRIST
IN PROCESS HERMENEUTIC
  by Russell Pregeant
ENCOUNTER WITH THE TEXT: FORM AND HISTORY IN
THE HEBREW BIBLE
  edited by Martin J. Buss
FINDING IS THE FIRST ACT: TROVE FOLK TALES
AND JESUS' TREASURE PARABLE
  by John Dominic Crossan
THE BIBLICAL MOSAIC: CHANGING PERSPECTIVES
  edited by Robert M. Polzin and Eugene Rothman
SEMANTICS OF NEW TESTAMENT GREEK
  by J. P. Louw

THE WORKINGS
OF OLD TESTAMENT
NARRATIVE

Peter D. Miscall

FORTRESS PRESS
Philadelphia, Pennsylvania

SCHOLARS PRESS
Chico, California

Library of Congress Cataloging in Publication Data

Miscall, Peter D.

  The workings of Old Testament narrative.

  (Semeia studies)
  Bibliography: p. 147
  1. Bible. O.T.—Criticism, interpretation, etc. I. Title. II. Series.
BS1171.2.M57 1983   222′.11066   82-48570
ISBN 0-8006-1512-3 (Fortress Press)
ISBN 0-89130-584-X (Scholars Press)   AACR2

9766K82   Printed in the United States of America   1-1512

To Rev. George Barry
who first led me into the Bible

Although I wrote this book in the first part of 1980, much work and thought preceded the actual writing. I am indebted to a large number of my students and colleagues who have contributed in many ways to this work. In particular I want to acknowledge the help and support I received from Burton Feldman, Stephen Doty, and Eric Gould. I am also grateful to Burton Feldman for making it possible for me to spend my sabbatical in winter, 1980, at the English Department of the University of Denver.

Contents

INTRODUCTION

Reading

The readings contained in this work deal with the richness, complexity, and elusiveness of OT narrative and also with its concreteness and detail. The two sets of qualities can appear contradictory since the latter qualities should produce clear and well-defined stories and characters, not ones that are elusive. However, it is my contention that OT narrative is complex and elusive because of, not in spite of, the concrete details. There is, at the same time, too little and too much of the narrative, too few and too many details, and this gives rise to the many, and frequently contradictory, interpretations of and conjectures about OT narrative. It is this mode of biblical narrative that I wish to display partially and to account for, and I will do so by a close reading of selected passages from Genesis and 1 Samuel.

This part of the threefold introduction is a presentation of what I intend by the term reading. The other two parts are discussions of some aspects of the arrangement and style of OT narrative that impinge directly upon a reading. Detailed examples are developed in the readings in the body of the work.

My approach is close reading. I focus on the text in its specificity and its entirety. Although I treat in detail a few sections selected from Genesis and 1 Samuel, I regard them as part of the larger corpus Genesis–2 Kings, which presents a connected story going from the creation to the early days of Israel's exile. This is the work, the "book," parts of which I discuss. The restriction of focus to Genesis–2 Kings is justified in part by the shared plot, themes, style, etc., of the corpus and also by personal background and choice. Genesis–2 Kings is enough for now. However, I do not intend the restriction to mean that I will defend the corpus, now or in the future, as a separate and independent work in the OT.

The text, in the sense both of the individual passage or passages that I am reading and of the entire corpus, is a material entity consisting of specific words in a particular arrangement. The readings respect the specificity and pay close attention to what exactly is said, how it is said, and also note what is not said, what the text leaves out. This respect extends to all of the details, oddities, gaps, etc., of the text. I do not remove troublesome details and statements by explaining them away in some fashion or by ignoring them; they remain even though they block a coherent and definitive interpretation. Nor do I try to fill in worrisome lacunae by bringing information from another part of the text or by conjecture; they stay empty even though they also prevent a definitive interpretation. Reading a passage is not to reduce it to, or to replace it with, themes, character portrayals, history, some "deep structure," or such. Reading is to follow the text, to trace its workings, even if it turns out that it is undecidable.

"Undecidable": the reading encounters ambiguity, equivocation, opposed meanings and cannot decide for or establish one or the other; the reading cannot stop, it cannot control or limit the text. The analysis of the David and Goliath story provides a good illustration, and I simplify the discussion better to focus on the notion of undecidability (see below pp. 60–62). I argue at length that David's character is undecidable. The text permits us to regard David as a pious and innocent young shepherd going to battle the Philistine because of the latter's defiance of the Lord and as a cunning and ambitious young warrior who is aware of the effects that his defeat of Goliath will have on the assembled army, i.e., as a "good" and a "bad" David. Biblical commentaries and studies decide the issue, usually in favor of the former portrayal, although arguments in favor of the latter are not unheard of. However, regardless of the specific portrayal, the assumption is that David is being portrayed in some specifiable, some definitive, fashion, i.e., ultimately David is "good" *or* "bad."

This is where I locate the undecidability, the indeterminateness: David is not being portrayed in a definitive fashion. David is "good" *and* "bad." The text at the same time supports both and does not support a final decision in favor of only one. In the analysis, undecidability marks the attempt to demonstrate that David is both good and bad, that the text of 1 Samuel 17 supports both views at the same time. It is not an attempt to argue for a "new" interpretation of David.

The reading of a given passage also takes into account parallel material found elsewhere in Genesis–2 Kings. "Parallel" and "analogy" are not used in a restricted sense. I do not argue that parallel passages which I have grouped are connected because they share an underlying genre, archetype, motif, or other general category. So to argue would be to suppress many of the specifics of each passage. By a parallel or analogous text, I mean any other passage that I can compare and contrast, in whatever way, with the passage under consideration. I establish parallels in one or more of a variety of ways, e.g., similarity of plot, of theme, of configuration of characters, and of terminology and phraseology. The purpose is not to provide a foundational pattern, but is to relate passages, different parts of the corpus of Genesis–2 Kings, in order to enrich the reading of one part and of the entire corpus.

Parallels relate to the repetition that is characteristic of OT narrative, repetition that ranges from the "same story" being told two or more times, to similar stories being told, to material that repeats a speech, a description, or such, or that shares some pattern, themes, characters, vocabulary and phraseology, etc./1/. The reading takes such repetition into account and relates it to the richness and openness of OT narrative.

I have no expectation that parallel and analogous passages will "clear things up" and help produce a consistent and definitive reading. Even though I do focus on a given section of the text, this is for practical purposes and is not to privilege it, to make it primary, so that any parallels will serve only to explicate it, i.e., to make the parallel passage(s) secondary, accessory. Parallel passages are dealt with in their entirety and specificity and are not reduced to just those elements that they have in common with each other and with the "primary" text, to just those elements that help elucidate the "primary" text. Analogous passages are part of the same text, and the influence, the effect, the significance of an analogy will not go just one way and will not be restricted to just "helpful" aspects. Parallel sections are mutually parallel; one is not primary and privileged. I do not restrict myself only to using a clearer and more explicit section to help illuminate and clarify a more obscure and elliptical passage. The effect can go the other way; the clearer passage can be clouded when compared with the more problematic section.

Indeed, it is not my goal in reading OT narrative to produce and support any type of univocal, definitive meaning or understanding. OT narrative is too complex and evasive for that. My reading traces the workings of the text even when the reading becomes indeterminable and undecidable. To borrow an image from J. Hillis Miller, I follow the various threads of the text, but as Ariadne's thread, they do not lead to the center of the labyrinth, rather they construct it (1978). My reading does not produce answers or definitive meanings; it does not go to the center or "the heart" of the biblical text; rather it produces more questions as it plays upon and with the multifarious aspects of biblical narrative.

This is a departure from the major ways of reading the Bible, especially reading with the desire for clarity, definition, the essential, the true, the final determination of "what it really means." In such a reading, there is little or no toleration for inconsistency and contradiction, which must be ignored, denied, removed, or in some fashion overcome. The assumption is that there is an essential meaning, a true core, or a purpose and an intention, that is to be obtained by variously "stripping away" or "cutting through" the outer layers of the text which can be termed historical, mythic, literary, or such. Whatever they are called, the point is that the text, with all its details, oddities, and lacunae, is seen as an obstacle that must be overcome or removed to reach the essential meaning or meanings that are within or beyond the text.

But the text in its entirety and specificity does not support such essentialist reading. The reactions to the biblical text with its manifold difficulties, inconsistencies, and even contradictions, have been to suppress the text itself in some fashion in favor of a univocal reading or interpretation, usually historical or theological, or to rend the text into sources, fragments, "genres," etc., which can then supposedly support definitive meaning. This is not my mode of reading.

I will digress several times from my readings to discuss specific examples drawn from commentaries on Genesis and 1 Samuel of how the biblical text is suppressed, ignored, or denied, and I therefore now restrict myself to a few introductory comments. By "univocal reading or interpretation" I mean that a commentator, faced with a biblical text that is multi-layered, troublesome, ambiguous, or equivocal responds by asserting that such is the basic meaning, the main intention, the essential teaching, etc., of the text. The text, according to this mode of argument, may have several or many viable interpretations, and each one can be stated definitively and clearly. Each of the several interpretations may then be assigned to different methods or approaches, e.g., historical, literary, or theological, or there may be some argument in favor of one interpretation as the best, the most probable, the most preferred, etc.

On the other hand, the assertion of one interpretation is frequently made without supporting arguments as though it were self-evident, and other aspects and details of the text that do not accord with it or that support other interpretations are in some way ignored or denied significance for the basic meaning. The basic meaning can be of any type and is dependent on the particular desires and methods of the commentator. Such a response characterizes commentaries ranging from conservative and orthodox to liberal and historical-critical. Again, this is not my mode of reading. I am not attempting to develop a new interpretation either as *the* interpretation or as one more to be added to an already lengthy list of interpretations of Abraham and David.

I cite passages from specific commentaries, not because the commentaries are faulty or wrong, but because they are highly regarded within their respective areas. They are very good commentaries and therefore offer excellent examples of the modes of reading the OT that I am departing from. However, the historical-critical approach, for example, does not exist as an abstract method that can be criticized in itself; there are only individual commentaries that employ, in their own limited fashion, the historical-critical approach. Therefore my comments and criticisms do concern specific commentaries and quotations from them, and the criticisms are at times harsh. Whether because of some methodological or other shortcoming, I find that biblical commentaries frequently miss what is there, posit what is not there, or make naive literary assumptions about narrative and its modes, e.g., of plot development and character portrayal. I give examples in the body of the work.

Finally, I cite from commentaries to give examples of what I am not doing with the hope that this will better present what I am trying to do. I am not attempting a full reading and analysis of biblical commentaries, of whatever persuasion, nor of any methodology displayed by commentaries. Such reading and analysis awaits extensive future study. Indeed, I only hint at the implications of my work in the areas of biblical theology, history, and such.

The Arrangement of the Text

The dominant arrangement of Genesis–2 Kings and of each of its separate episodes, sections, and books is a linear chronology from the time of creation to the final note on Jehoiachin's care in Babylon. However, the chronological framework is not strict as there are many sections that anticipate the following narrative, that present "flashbacks" to and retrospectives on the preceding narrative, or whose exact chronological placement cannot be decided/2/. Further, events, episodes, sections will be narrated and presented one after the other, in linear sequence, but frequently with no explicit indication of any relation between them beyond the temporal one. Even then, the amount of time elapsed may not be specified. "After these things, such-and-such happened." In many instances, even a temporal relation is lacking leaving the reader free to play with possibilities.

Examples are found in the Abraham Cycle. Gen 12:17–18: "The Lord afflicted Pharaoh . . . and Pharaoh summoned Abram . . ."/3/. There is a causal or necessary relation between the affliction and the summoning; there is only a chance or coincidental relation. I am not asserting an either/or choice, but both/and at the same time; the issue is undecidable. In any case, the problem stems from the narration of two events in narrative sequence with no indication of any relation between them other than temporal sequence.

Genesis 14 comes between 13 and 15, and its relation to them has been the object of lengthy study and debate. It comes temporally between the events of 13 and 15, i.e., it is here because "that's the way it happened"; it is unrelated to 13 and 15 and has been placed here by chance. Again, both necessity and chance are supported by the text. Even if one leaves aside the issue of temporal or causal connections between Genesis 14 and its context, the reader can still toy with the possibility of thematic and even verbal relations/4/. Indeed, one can "move" the chapter out of its context; perhaps its events transpired later and are narrated here out of strict chronological sequence. It could occur anytime before the events of Genesis 18–19 when Sodom and Gomorrah are destroyed and after which Abraham moves from Mamre. In this example, the narrative sequence does not even assure a temporal sequence.

A chronological overview of the Abraham Cycle reveals that some events are specifically dated: the departure from Haran (Gen 12:4), the births of Ishmael and Isaac (16:16; 21:5), the second covenant (17:1), and the deaths of Abraham and Sarah (25:7; 23:1). This provides a tight chronological system, but with large and noticeable gaps which are treated in different ways in the narration. There are eleven years from the departure until the birth of Ishmael into which are fitted the events of Genesis 12–13, 15–16, and presumably 14. This is five chapters for eleven years. (It is noteworthy that the first covenant with Abraham in Genesis 15 is undated; it occurred "after these things" [15:1].) There is a thirteen year gap between the birth of Ishmael (16:16) and the second covenant with Abraham (17:1). Nothing is narrated of the period, i.e., no chapters for thirteen years. The events of Gen 17:1–21:7 occupy approximately one year, from the forecast of Isaac's birth (17:15–21) to the birth itself (21:1–7). This is a little more than four chapters for one year. The next time post is Sarah's death, thirty-seven years after Isaac's birth (23:1). All that is narrated of the period are the happenings of 21:8–22:24 which include the sacrifice of Isaac. (As with Genesis 15, it is noteworthy that the latter event also is undated, occurring "after these things" [22:1].) This is a little less than two chapters for thirty-seven years. The tight, explicit chronological framework emphasizes the gaps and the undated events/5/.

After Sarah's death, Abraham purchases a tomb site for her, obtains a wife for Isaac, has other children, but sends them away from Isaac (25:6); he then dies. Not much for his last thirty-eight years; this is a little over two chapters for thirty-eight years. However, this is deceptive. It must be noted that Abraham's death, as that of Isaac in 35:28–29, is narrated in anticipation since Abraham has fifteen years of life left at the time of the birth of Esau and Jacob (25:25). The text gives the impression that Abraham died long before their birth. A reading of the full Abraham and Jacob stories will have to take these points into account.

The Style of the Text

The style of OT narrative is consistent in its use of "matter-of-fact," "clear," and "literal" terminology, descriptions, and narration. There is seldom much trouble in determining what OT narrative is narrating or describing even though the significance for the overall narrative of what is narrated or described may be difficult to determine, if it can be determined at all. The war of the kings in Gen 14:1–12 is a good example of clarity of description and narration and yet opaqueness of significance, especially if one attempts to relate it to its context. OT narrative infrequently employs similes, metaphors, and other common figures of speech; events are told "literally."

I have put the above terms in quotation marks for two reasons. First, the words have a rich range of meaning and a lengthy history of use in our traditions of reading and interpretation. I want to restrict them to the connotation of non-figural, non-symbolic discourse without positing a strict opposition between "literal" and "figurative" (metaphorical) language. For me the distinction is one of degree rather than one of essence; it is a practical, empirical issue. "Asahel was as swift of foot as a wild gazelle" (2 Sam 2:18). The statement is striking since OT narrative seldom uses an "as" or a "like" followed by a comparative term. David is a shepherd and a man of war who claims to have fought lions and bears (1 Sam 17:34–37), but with one exception (2 Sam 17:8), David is not described as a lion in war or as fighting like a bear. The "literal" aspect of OT narrative can be grasped by comparing it with poetic discourse and its consistent use of metaphors and other figures of speech. 2 Sam 22, especially the opening theophany, is an excellent example of the latter.

Second, the terms, particularly "literal" and "matter-of-fact," are frequently equated with other possible terms like "realistic" and "history-like." However, there is a problem inherent in their application to OT narrative since a realistic, history-like narrative does not include God, angels, miracles, etc. OT narrative narrates divine actions, speeches, miracles, etc., as literally, as matter-of-factly, as it does so-called realistic or history-like events and people/6/. I restrict the terms to the narrative and descriptive style and do not equate literal with "historical," "real," "true." The question of historicity is not addressed in this book since it is outside the range of my present interests.

Nevertheless, OT narrative does have a metaphorical aspect if we understand metaphor in its "paradigmatic" and "substitutive" sense, i.e., the metaphor on the page can be seen as a "substitute" for another word or words; it belongs to a "paradigm." I have already noted that there are many types of repetition in biblical narrative and that it is a very frequent phenomenon. This results in a parallel or parallels of some variety to every individual episode, story, description, etc. It can be said that each of the latter belongs to a "paradigm," i.e., there are other episodes, stories, descriptions, etc., that are similar and that must be taken into account in reading. Each, in some sense, is a "substitute" for another possible text or texts; an entire passage, and not just a word or phrase, can be considered metaphorical.

The metaphorical or paradigmatic quality can derive from an individual episode in its relations to other parallels, e.g., Gen 12:10–20 and the analogous stories in Genesis 20 and 26, or from its possible relations to its immediate context, e.g., 12:10–20 in Genesis 12–13. Does 12:10–20 correspond to or contrast with its context? Or,

in terms of character, is the Abraham of 12:10-20 the same as, or
different from, the Abraham of 12:1-9 and 13:1-18? The effect, the
questions, derive from the previously mentioned fact that OT narrative narrates episodes one after the other with little or no indication of the relationship(s) between them. The paradigmatic aspect
of biblical narrative interferes with the simple literality and linear-
ity of the text being read by adding a surplus to it, by showing that
more is involved than just the given passage.

The interpretive move begun within the passage is further fueled
by the paradigmatic aspect. It spurs the attempt to locate some
overarching pattern or patterns, some meaning or meanings, that will
account for the single text both in its specificity and in its relations to
the rest of the biblical narrative, and yet the specificity, both details
and lacunae, of the single text and of the rest of the biblical narrative
block the fulfillment of the task. Patterns and meanings are established, but they are not total or exhaustive; "parts" of the text will
have to be left out; there will always be a residue.

> The question of a reading's "truth" must be at least compli-
> cated and re-thought through another question, which
> Freud, indeed, has raised, and taught us to articulate: what
> does such "truth" (or any truth) leave out? What is it *made
> to miss*? What does it have as its function to overlook?
> What, precisely, is its residue, the *remainder* it does not
> account for? (Felman: 117; her italics)

NOTES

/1/   See Alter, "Biblical Narrative," for an excellent discussion.

/2/   For example: there is anticipation in Gen 15:13-16 and a "flashback" in Gen 15:7. For discussion of the latter, see Weiss, "Weiteres über
die Bauformen des Erzählens in der Bibel."

/3/   In my text, I employ Abraham and Sarah regardless of the reference in Genesis. In citations, I use Abram and Sarai when they occur in the
biblical text. Quotes are generally cited from the *RSV*; at times I do change
the translation to a more "literal" rendering or to a rendering that better
displays a parallel with another text.

/4/   For example, see the following studies of Genesis 38 which
relate it to its context by associations of word, theme, and structure: Alter,
"A Literary Approach to The Bible," pp. 73-76, and Seybold, "Paradox and
Symmetry in the Joseph Narrative."

/5/   I generally employ the following distinctions in "dated" events: explicitly dated; undated yet calculable; and a "gap" which is uncalculable.

/6/   See Frei, *The Eclipse of Biblical Narrative*, especially pp. 1–16 and 124–54, and Zuck, "Tales of Wonder: Biblical Narrative, Myth and Fairy Stories."

PART I
GENESIS 12 AND RELATED TEXTS

Introduction

The Abraham narrative in Gen 11:10–25:18 is of a highly epi-
sodic nature. Each story, to some extent, stands on its own, and its
contribution and relation to the rest of the narrative is not extensive,
if any relation or contribution is at all apparent. Even the chronology, pertaining to both the order of events and the amount of time
involved in an event or elapsed between events, is not always
apparent or calculable despite the fact that the time-frame for the
entire Abraham cycle and some of its major events is given in the
narration. This, as in the examples in the Introduction, leads a
reader to assume or to establish by some means the relation of a
given episode to its context. However, the text does not provide
enough information, and at the same time it provides too much
information, to resolve definitively the issues and thereby leaves the
reader free to play. The following readings of Genesis 12 are meant
to exemplify the play. First, some selected points in Gen 12:1–9 are
treated, and then there is a more sustained and thorough reading of
Gen 12:10–20 and material related to it.

Genesis 12:1–9: There, But Not Here

The call of Abraham in 12:1–9 is narrated with attention to
detail, but we are told only what Abraham does. He does not speak,
and nothing is said of his reaction to the Lord's two speeches in vss.
1–3 and 7, if he had any reactions. As noted in the Introduction, a
reader will tend not to remain satisfied with just a narration of
Abraham's acts and God's speeches, but will want to posit specific
relations between the two and then infer something about Abraham's character based on the posited relations. In most commentaries on Genesis, this takes the form of Abraham the faithful who
responds to the call immediately and without question. But, given

only the text, the understanding is based on the assumption *post hoc ergo propter hoc*, and it also sets up a contrast with 12:10–20 which depicts a less-than-faithful Abraham who readily leaves the land which was so central to the preceding narrative. I emphasize that this is not to claim that the assumption mentioned above about 12:1–9 is wrong, but that it is not explicitly supported by the text as the only or as the best interpretation.

Gen 12:4: "And Abram went as the Lord had told him." Is the "as" equivalent to "because" as in many translations, or is this a type of "verbal simile" which comments on Abraham's going by informing us that he went from his country, his kindred, and his father's house (see 12:1), but tells us nothing about why? Abraham is completing the migration begun by his father: "Terah took Abram his son . . . and they went forth together from Ur of the Chaldeans to go into the land of Canaan; but when they came to Haran, they settled there" (11:31). The text itself has provided another motivation for Abraham's leaving and going to Canaan.

The particle "as" (Heb: *ka'ăšer*) is frequently used to point to a congruence between a course of action and a previous statement without positing a necessary causal relation, i.e., a phrase such as "as the Lord said" can be shorthand for describing the action and not the character's motivation/1/. It may mean "because" in some places, but there are other prepositions in Hebrew that denote "because" or "on account of." Three of them are used, for a total of four times, in 12:13–17, perhaps emphasizing that the preposition in vs. 4 does not mean "because." The syntax and the context prevent the definitive conclusion that Abraham went solely in response to the Lord's command; at the same time, the syntax and the context prevent the definitive conclusion that Abraham went for his own reasons and not in response to the Lord's command.

There are several other important texts that can help with the problem. First is Gen 22:1–3:

> After these things God tested Abraham, and said to him, "Abraham!" And he said, "Here am I." He said, "Take your son, your only son Isaac, whom you love, and go to the land of Moriah, and offer him there as a burnt offering upon one of the mountains of which I shall tell you." So Abraham rose early in the morning, saddled his ass, and took two of his young men with him, and his son Isaac; and he cut the wood for the burnt offering, and arose and went to the place of which God had told him.

Abraham is again given a command by God to go, and this time he does respond quickly, "in the morning," and without question. There is no reason here to posit some other explanation for Abraham's behavior than God's command. Is this what happened in Genesis 12? Cassuto develops the parallel between 12:1-4 and 22:1-3 and concludes that "in both cases Abram undergoes an ordeal . . . Abram, like Noah in his day, fulfilled the command given him by the Almighty. The Lord said to him, '*Go*,' and *he went*" (310, 316; his italics).

I am here arguing that one reason a reader will posit a causal relation between God's command in 12:1-3 and Abraham's going in 12:4 is that the pattern of divine call and immediate, unquestioning response explicitly occurs with him at another point in the narrative. In Genesis 22, as in Genesis 12, the narration provides no hint as to Abraham's reaction to or feelings about God's command. But, in this instance, there is reason to expect some such information from the narration since it previously informed us that when Sarah demanded that he expel Hagar and Ishmael, "the thing was very displeasing to Abraham *on account of his son*"(22:11; my italics; in the rest of the paper, italics will usually be mine; I will note only original italics).

The same narrative technique is at work between Genesis 12 and 22, and 22 and 21. A parallel text provides information that is not given in the first text and thereby leads the reader to wonder about its absence or even to posit its presence, although not explicitly mentioned, in the first text. In the Introduction, I noted that attention is drawn to the covenant story in Genesis 15 and to the sacrifice of Isaac in Genesis 22 because both happened "after these things," whereas many other events, in contradistinction, are dated to specific years in Abraham's life. It is what I term the "there, but not here" effect of analogies in OT narrative. I attempt to fill in narrative lacunae not just because they are there and I want a fuller, more explicit story, but also because there are parallels within the corpus itself that do not have the same lacunae and that apparently offer the information necessary to fill in the gap or gaps in the first text. Vice versa, the presence of a parallel or parallels that do not have the same gap or gaps emphasizes that the lacunae in the first text are deliberate, and the attempt to supply the information from elsewhere in the corpus or by conjecture can circumvent the intention of the text. From another standpoint, I can say that OT narrative is hereby commenting on itself, that the text itself is trying to show how it should be read.

Another aspect of the narrative technique is present in the examples. This is what I call the "branching process" by which the search for clarifying parallels leads to an increasing number of analogous passages, each of which is accompanied by its own problems and each of which has its own set of parallels, and so on. The search results, not in parallels that definitively resolve the beginning problem, but in a network of parallels, a web of analogies. The separate analogous passages compare and contrast with one another in manifold ways, and the result of following the network is not the center, the beginning, or the end, but the construction of a more elaborate network without center, beginning, or end.

To return to the parallels to Gen 12:1–4. At two different times, Abraham makes explicit reference to God's call. The first is in Gen 20:13. Abraham has passed Sarah off as his sister for the second time; this time to Abimelech king of Gerar. After God has informed him of the deception, Abimelech summons Abraham and rebukes him in strong terms.

> What have you done to us? And how have I sinned against you, that you have brought on me and on my kingdom a great sin? You have done to me things that ought not to be done . . . What were you thinking of, that you did this thing? (20:9–10)

Abraham replies at length and in three parts:

> (11) I did it because I thought, There is no fear of God at all in this place, and they will kill me because of my wife. (12) Besides she is indeed my sister, the daughter of my father but not the daughter of my mother; and she became my wife. (13) And when God caused me to wander from my father's house, I said to her, "This is the kindness you must do me: at every place to which we come, say of me, He is my brother." (20:11–13)

For now my focus is on the statement "when God caused me to wander from my father's house." The statement itself and its context do not inspire confidence that it expresses Abraham's beliefs about his departure from Haran.

First, God's command in 12:1–3 is specific and refers to Abraham's going to a place that God will show him; God does not "cause him to wander." Second, in Genesis 20, Abraham makes no effective response to Abimelech since only his opening statement directly answers one of Abimelech's questions, "What were you thinking of, that you did this thing?" The other two statements of Abraham are irrelevant to the situation. Or perhaps this is arrogance since Abraham does ignore most of Abimelech's questions and answers Pharaoh's which were asked the first time Abraham was caught in the lie about Sarah:

> What is this that you have done to me? Why did you not tell me that she was your wife? Why did you say, "She is my sister," so that I took her for my wife? (12:18–19)

Indeed, Abraham's third excuse in vs. 13, ". . . *at every place* to which we come, say of me, He is my brother," contradicts his first statement in vs. 11, "I did it because I thought, There is no fear of God at all *in this place* . . . ," unless the latter is taken as a general motivation, i.e., Abraham thinks "there is no fear of God" in any place that he comes to. The third statement can also be an indirect effort to shift the blame to God. Such a lame or arrogant reply does not lead us to trust its explicit statements which include Abraham's claim that Sarah is at least his half-sister, "the daughter of my father but not the daughter of my mother."

Many commentaries and studies take Abraham's claims as "true," particularly the claim that Sarah is his half-sister. For von Rad, it is not even Abraham's claim, but "the opinion of our narrator."

> . . . in the opinion of our narrator Sarah was really Abraham's half sister. Marriage with one's half sister was forbidden by later law (Lev 18:9, 11; 20:17) but was still possible at the time of David (2 Sam 13:13). This notation (20:12) must therefore be ancient tradition. (von Rad, 222; see also Vawter, 181; Speiser, 149–150; Skinner, 318; *et. al.*)

Such an acceptance of Abraham's statements reflects a naive treatment of character portrayal; no attention is given to the circumstances in which the statement is made. No question about its trustworthiness is even raised.

The second mention of God's call of Abraham is in Genesis 24. Abraham sends his servant back to Haran to obtain a wife for Isaac; in his charge to the servant, he refers to "the Lord, the God of heaven, who took me from my father's house and from the land of my birth, and who spoke to me and swore to me, 'To your descendants I will give this land,'" (24:7). Here the statement with its reminiscences of Gen 12:1–9 and the context leave less room to doubt that Abraham regards his migration from Haran as the work of the Lord. Indeed, God himself has previously confirmed the fact for Abraham: "I am the Lord who brought you from Ur of the Chaldeans, to give you this land to possess" (15:7).

Still, there is some reason for doubt as this is a formal commissioning of the servant, and Abraham's statement in vs. 7 may only be appropriate to the occasion or may be just an attempt to give the servant added confidence that his mission will succeed. Yet, in any case, what we would have certainty of in the passage is Abraham's belief in God's guidance at an advanced stage in his life and not what he felt or believed sixty or more years before. Finally, Abraham's statement is that "the Lord took him," not that the Lord called and consequently he went. Thus neither Genesis 20 nor 24 can confirm that Abraham responded directly to the divine call in Genesis 12. Let us go beyond Genesis for "evidence."

There are three other major "call narratives" in Genesis–2 Kings, i.e., calls that come directly from God and not through some intermediary. The three are the call of Moses in Exodus 3–4, of Gideon in Judges 6–7, and of Samuel in 1 Samuel 3. I discuss them only as they can be associated with the call of Abraham, and my treatment is general. The four call stories form a paradigm, and yet because the specific differences outweigh the similarities, I do not reduce them to one pattern, to an ideal paradigm or "genre."

Moses is called and commissioned by God to bring the people out of Egypt. Moses goes in response, but only after he raises several objections and God has responded to them. The first two objections concern Moses himself and God. "Who am I that I should go to Pharaoh, and bring the sons of Israel out of Egypt?" (Exod 3:11). The second asks for the name of the God who is sending Moses, i.e., "Who are you?" (see 3:13). Gideon, on the other hand, responds by asking for proof, in the form of signs or miracles, that it is God in fact who is calling him, and then he acts fearfully or only in accordance with the specific instructions of God. This is not unquestioning, unqualified response. Samuel at first does not even realize that it is the Lord who is calling him; it is Eli who perceives it. The Lord tells Samuel what he is about to do to Eli's house, but he gives him no charge or commission. Samuel has to do nothing with the message; he has no response to make.

Thus, it is impossible to use one or more of the four calls to "prove" something in another of the call narratives. However, the suggestions are rich, especially when we compare the terse account of Gen 12:1–9 with the lengthier stories of Moses, Gideon, and

Samuel. Does Abraham have anything in common with one or more of the three? Does Abraham question his own ability or worthiness to respond to God's call? Does he wonder who this Lord is who is calling to him? Does he need some sign that it is in fact God who is speaking to him? I can only ponder the questions and their implications; I cannot give final, definitive answers. The text does not support them. Gen 12:1–9 is too terse, too laconic, and the parallels cited provide too many analogies, too many possibilities.

Abraham is leaving Haran in faith and obedience to God's call; he is leaving for some other reason or reasons that have nothing to do with God's command. If we assume the former and see "Abraham the faithful," then there is a problem with interpreting the contrast that is thereby established with Abraham in 12:10–20 who acts without consulting the Lord, who lies, and who allows his wife to enter into an adulterous situation. The problem has been addressed and dealt with in commentaries, and I will present some of their solutions later.

On the other hand, there is no contrast since the ambiguity of Gen 12:1–9 is settled by 12:10–20. Abraham in Genesis 12 is a consistent, coherent character, an opportunist who will take advantage of any situation and of anyone, including God. Abraham is leaving Haran for his own personal reasons and is doing so now with the hope of gaining some benefit from the Lord. The portrayal continues into Genesis 13. Abraham proposes the choice of land to Lot knowing that Lot, in his rashness, will choose by appearances. Or, Abraham does not care which section of land he gets, and Lot is given a true choice. Abraham had previously left Canaan to go to Egypt despite God's promise to him that the former would be given to his descendants.

Character Portrayal

The paradigmatic play of biblical narrative is one of the mainstays of its richness and elusiveness and contributes thereby to the portrayal of characters. Robert Alter has raised the issue of characterization in OT narrative in his article, "Character in The Bible." He notes a discrepancy between readers' responses to biblical characters as vibrant and memorable and the textual portrayal of them in very sparse and external terms. We are told what people say and do; seldom do we get an "inner view" of their thoughts, emotions, motives, etc., or an "outer view" of their physical appearance. Therefore, we cannot explain biblical characterization as a portrayal in psychological depth and fullness.

Alter proposes a theory of biblical character portrayal based on the information about a character provided by biblical narrative, information which can be evaluated according to a scale of increasing certitude. At the point of lowest certitude, of inference, are a character's actions where we know only what a person does, not why she does it or what she is feeling and thinking. Gen 12:1–9 is a good example. In the middle of the scale are a character's statements and the statements of others about her; here we have expressions of thought and motivation which we can judge and weigh. The latter must take into account the general setting in which the statements are made since it can seriously influence our appraisal of the statement's trustworthiness. This was the procedure I followed with the passages cited from Genesis 20 and 24. The upper end of the scale is the omniscient narrator's statements of character's intentions, motivations, feelings, etc. Gen 21:11 is the only example cited so far.

Given the scale, Alter emphasizes the narrator's careful and selective use of these ways of portraying a personage, particularly the ways that yield certainty. He exemplifies the approach via a reading of the story of David and Michal. He notes that although we are frequently informed of Michal's feelings and motives, e.g., she loves David, we are told nothing of David's reciprocal feelings. We are left with a choice of sincere love, political ambition, or some combination of them, but the narrator does not give enough information with which to make a sure choice. The observation applies to almost all of David's dealings with Saul and his family; we are told their emotions, intentions, and such, but with a few exceptions, we are told nothing of David's feelings, intentions, or such.

Alter's theory is a specific example of the general narrative technique discussed above. The reader's attention is drawn to the lack of specific information in one passage because of its presence in a second context that is similar to the first. Indeed, reflection upon Alter's work has been influential in the development of my understanding of the "there, but not here" effect. However, there are some serious problems with Alter's approach and some limitations to its applicability.

First, although I have not done much research on the issue of the narrator, either in terms of mode or voice, I do find biblical narrative too diverse and changing even to speak of a narrator, let alone an "omniscient narrator." OT narrative changes too frequently and too sharply in style of narration and description, in vision, etc., for me to talk of a narrator who is altering his style and view of things/2/. Therefore I use the impersonal terms narrative, text, narration, etc.

Second, Alter's analysis is effective on the specific material that he treats, but it cannot be assumed that it will be just as effective on other sections of biblical narrative including other parts of the David story. For example, in the Abraham story, we are seldom told of anyone's thoughts, feelings, motivations, etc., and therefore cannot do the same type of character analysis as Alter does with the David and Michal story.

More seriously, I do not think that OT narrative differs only in its literary mode of character portrayal, but also in its "understanding" of human character and personality, if the latter terms are themselves relevant to the people encountered in the OT and if narrative, in any sense of the term, can be spoken of as having "understanding." Even though I may at times use the terms for want of others, I have serious reservations about the applicability of words such as motivation and intention. Not because they do not have some relevance to biblical characterization, but because of the extensive psychological and philosophical implications that their use entails. Biblical narrative does not necessarily have to have much in common with modern, Western psychological theories and models of personality and all of the terminology involved in them. At present I think that the very words character and personality, as developed in Western literature, theology, psychology, etc., are misleading as they are defined through concepts such as centered self, will, motivation, etc. My reading of OT narrative has found no correspondence to such a theory of character. But I do not intend this pejoratively since biblical narrative does in fact portray people. The present problem is to describe how without judging the portrayal and understanding of a human being as primitive and superficial, and without assuming that it somehow must correspond to a modern psychological theory that is regarded as "true."

As Alter notes, OT narrative does not give much information, if any, on motives, intentions, feelings, etc., therefore maybe these are only a small part of the understanding of a human person, or perhaps such information is to be read in terms other than motives and intentions. However, as small a part as they might play and whatever we wish to term them, "motives," "intentions," "feelings" are noted at times in the biblical text and cannot be ignored. And if they are noted in only a few places, we will still want to ascribe them to other characters in other places. If they are there, then why not here?

In the same article, Alter speaks of "an abiding mystery in character," of "the capacity for change exhibited by the biblical personages who are treated at any length." He then asserts that

> this unpredictable and changing nature of character is one reason why biblical personages cannot have fixed Homeric epithets . . . but only relational epithets determined by the strategic requirements of the immediate context. (64)

I agree and, at the same time, want to raise the more radical question whether the very term "character" is appropriate to biblical narrative. For, even if a biblical character is called "unpredictable and changing," there is still something, some core, some center, that is unpredictable, that changes. The point is Nietzsche's.

> Logical world-denial and nihilation follow from the fact that we have to oppose non-being with being and that the concept "becoming" is denied. ("*Something*" becomes.) (312; his italics)/3/

My reading of OT narrative not only does not produce certain, developed portrayals of a personage's inner motives and intentions, but it has given me no reason to think of a core, a central personality, a "something" for a depicted person. It is not that Abraham or David are unpredictable or wrapped in "an abiding mystery"; they are undecidable.

Biblical characterization is an aspect of biblical narrative and, as such, is part of the paradigmatic play of the narrative. Analogies add to character portrayal by confirming possibilities within the given text and by raising new ones, but as possibilities, alternatives, and not as evidence to "prove" that one, and only one, of the possibilities is the correct one or at least the most probable one. Biblical characterization, as part of biblical narrative, is also indeterminate, undecidable. The text, at the same time, provides too little and too much information for us to establish a definite portrait of a character even if we speak of it as a mystery, as "unpredictable and changing."

For example, in the preceding reading different motivations were ascribed to Abraham for leaving Haran and for proposing to Lot that he choose which land he will live in. The discussion of the latter could have been more complicated, especially if I had brought in the parallel conflict-resolution stories in Genesis 21 and 26, both of which express analogies to 12:10–20. Such attempts to establish specific motives and intentions introduce much of the working and play of OT narrative, but end in undecidability. The attempts do not result in the establishment of a few possible views of a character and of their motives and intentions. Even if the views are sharply contrasting or contradictory, they are still developed, centered portrayals. Abraham is either faithful and obedient or cunning and opportunistic. Given either one, a consistent reading can then be made of Genesis 12–13. However, I am asserting that it is not a matter of choosing either one or the other, but of choosing both and at the same time. Further, it is not a question of two, or some limited number of, alternatives, but of a continuum, of a spectrum in which one color imperceptibly merges into another. The two Abrahams are not two distinct possible characters, but positions at either end of the continuum of the person Abraham which are already merging into other possible characters and are moving towards each other.

In some instances the narrative may, at the same time, "clear things up" by definitively stating what has happened, by definitively ascribing some attribute, motive or such, to a given character, or by some other type of definitive assertion. For example, in the covenant narrative in Genesis 15, God gives Abraham a far more explicit geographical description of the land that he is giving to Abraham and his descendants than he gave to him at Shechem (12:7) and at Bethel (13:14–17). Second, after the many vicissitudes of his life, the narration informs us that "now Abraham was old, well advanced in years; and the Lord had blessed Abraham in all things" (24:1).

On the other hand, in just as many instances if not more, the continuing narrative will only add more acts and speeches that are susceptible to a wide range of interpretation. Each act and speech will be able to be read on its own continuum of interpretation. This will not decide any issues from previous episodes, but will add more undecidable features to a portrayal that is already complex and undecidable. I have already hinted at this in my comments on Genesis 12–13 and will develop it more fully in the following readings.

Even when the continuing narrative does establish some definite points, their significance for the overall narrative can be limited, sometimes quite severely. For example, the explicit description of the boundaries in Genesis 15 has little or no significance for the rest of the Abraham story or for the remainder of the book of Genesis. Indeed, extending the northern border to the Euphrates contrasts sharply with the actual extent of the land conquered later by Joshua and David. Finally, the description only tells us that at this point Abraham knows the borders; it tells us nothing of what he knew before this point or how he understood or reacted to the Lord's two previous promises of the land.

Second, the assertion in 24:1 that "the Lord had blessed Abraham in all things" provides a fact about Abraham, but it is not explicit about why the Lord blessed Abraham nor about how Abraham understands the blessing, if he even perceives that he has been blessed. Twice before the Lord has promised Abraham that he will bless him. "I will make of you a great nation, and I will bless you, and make your name great, so that you will be a blessing" (12:2). The second promise is more emphatic.

> By myself I have sworn, says the Lord, because you have done this, and have not withheld your son, your only son, *I will indeed bless you*, and I will multiply your descendants as the stars of heaven and as the sand which is on the sea-shore. And your descendants shall possess the gate of their enemies . . . because you have obeyed my voice. (22:16–18)

Here is a reason why the Lord will bless Abraham. Abraham has not withheld Isaac from him and has obeyed his voice. The two are apparently synonomous, but there is the possibility that Abraham's obedience includes more than just the near-sacrifice of Isaac. The notice that Abraham was in fact blessed by the Lord does not come until Sarah has died and Abraham has gone through negotiations to purchase the field of Machpelah so that he can bury her in the cave in the field (Genesis 23). Is this a further act of obedience by Abraham? Does the Lord's blessing hinge on the purchase and burial, or has the text provided the statement of blessing sometime after the fact? That is, Abraham was blessed soon after the near-sacrifice of Isaac and before the death of Sarah. The text, through its specific statements and arrangement, raises the questions, but does not answer them. The text supplies a "fact," but a fact whose significance is undecidable.

The phenomenon is encountered frequently in biblical characterization. "Facts" are provided, but with indeterminate significance. From another standpoint, although at times we can make statements of fact about a personage in the narrative, we cannot always turn them into judgments of character. Specific speeches, acts, themes, etc., can be associated with a given character, e.g., blessing with Abraham and violence with David, but their relation to a portrayal of the character remains open. For example, the story of David is replete with violence and blood; the theme of violence is undeniable, but what does it tell us of David? Is he therefore a brutal, violent man who murders all who get in his way, or is he a good man caught in the events of a turbulent time, unable to control the violence and brutality of those about him? In my reading, he is both and at the same time.

Genesis 12:10–20: Commentaries

I return now to Genesis 12, to the second tale, the narrative of Abraham and Sarah in Egypt. I have already commented on its possible associations with its context and now present some of the ways that commentaries have dealt with the passage, particularly in its context. This also demonstrates some of the modes of reading that I criticized in the Introduction.

One way is to deny implicitly any relationship between the story and its setting in Genesis 12–13. Since many, if not most, commentaries are divided into separate sections or chapters that deal with corresponding sections or episodes in the biblical text, it is very easy for a commentator to restrict himself to the passage at hand and to say little or nothing about what comes before or after. The denial is therefore implicit in that the commentary either ignores the context or makes only a few passing comments. Speiser, Sarna, and Vawter are excellent examples. Further, they ignore not just the specific biblical text, but also shift their analyses away from the specific biblical text to its analogies in Genesis 20 and 26 and to historical issues such as the proposed parallel with the Hurrian custom of adopting one's wife as one's sister to enhance her social status and the probability that Abraham, as a historical personage, actually went down to Egypt. Vawter, in fact, gives approximately twice as much space to the latter question as to the biblical text itself. Not only is the general context passed over, but the specific biblical text of Gen 12:10–20 is replaced by texts from Nuzi and Egypt and even by a lengthy passage from Albright (Vawter, 179–81).

Another approach is the explicit denial, or limitation, of any connections between the story and its setting. This is accomplished by source analytical argument concluding that 12:10–20 is from a different source or author than the rest of Genesis 12–13. This is the opinion of Gunkel and Skinner (Skinner, 251). A similar conclusion is that the tale was secondarily inserted into the main narrative by the Yahwist himself and therefore its relation to the main narrative is minimal. The view is espoused by von Rad (162–63) and Koch (115–17). Even Cassuto is close to the view with his theory that the story developed independently in oral tradition (337–40). The text at hand, Genesis 12–13, is replaced by at least two other texts, Gen 12:1–9 and 13:1–18, and 12:10–20, whose possible associations are denied or limited to a few theological principles; there is no attempt to analyze Genesis 12–13 in detail or as a single text.

For example, von Rad concludes his analysis of Genesis 12 by stating that "Yahweh does not allow his work [here the promises of 12:1–3 and 7] to miscarry right at the start; he rescues it and preserves it beyond all human failure" (164). This is particularly so when "the bearer of promise [is] himself the greatest enemy of the promise" (164). God's constant protection and the inevitable fulfillment of his purposes is a theological lesson frequently drawn from the narrative, e.g., it occurs in Skinner (250), Cassuto (337), Sarna (104), and Jacob (90) among others. Yet Yahweh's affliction of Pharaoh is not necessarily the cause of his awareness that Sarah is Abraham's wife, i.e., Abraham escaped from the situation by sheer luck. The Lord's constant protection is a possibility, but only a possibility, and to assert it as "the meaning" of the story is a form of univocal interpretation. One possible meaning is declared to be the main or only one; other possible interpretations are denied or, more frequently, ignored.

Others, especially those of a conservative persuasion, draw a different moral and religious lesson from the text. Cassuto, who goes to great length to exculpate Abraham of the charge that he hoped to get material gain by claiming Sarah as his sister, does accuse him of a lack of faith and of deception. He argues that the text is showing Abraham's conduct to be sinful by the punishment that is inflicted because of it (348–52). The same type of interpretation is found in Keil–Delitzsch (196–98). In one manner or another, Abraham is guilty of sin, but the moral lesson is thereby being taught that lack of faith in the Lord and reliance on human means ends in disaster. Here, again through univocal assertion, the specific text is reduced to, or replaced with, a moral lesson.

The question of Abraham's guilt, his lack of faith, in leaving the Promised Land without first turning to God for some guidance or protection is dependent on the reading of the foregoing narrative of Abraham in 12:1–9. Yet the specific sections of it read above were indeterminate in regard to Abraham's character. We are only told what he does, not why he does it, not what he says about it, nor how he reacts to it. The Lord commands Abraham to leave his home in Haran for a land that the Lord will show him. Abraham goes to Canaan, specifically to the northern city Shechem. The Lord appears again and tells Abraham, "To your descendants I will give this land" (12:7). Why did Abraham go from Haran, and why to Canaan? Did the Lord, in fact, somehow show him as he does in Genesis 22 (22:3)? Or is he just completing his father's original journey (Gen 11:31)? The text's silence on the point of why Canaan is striking. What does Abraham make of the Lord's command and of the particular promises contained within it? We can develop a scale of reactions, understandings, etc., in regard to each point raised by the questions, and the more issues that are added, the greater the complexity of Abraham, and the more numerous the aspects of his character that are undecidable.

The text does not authorize only a "good Abraham," a faithful and obedient man who accepts all that the Lord tells him and who will turn to the Lord for help in times of stress. Indeed, Abraham never speaks to the Lord without having first been spoken to; he never turns to the Lord for guidance in times of stress. If this is to be an indictment of Abraham in 12:10–20, then it is an indictment that applies to Abraham throughout his life. The topic of an individual's relation with God is in need of detailed investigation; I suspect that the indictment stems from our religious expectations and not biblical patterns.

Finally, is Abraham leaving the "Promised Land" or just Canaan, a land stricken with severe famine? At Shechem, the Lord said to Abraham, "*To your descendants* I will give *this land*." It is only later, at Bethel, that the Lord will say, "*all the land which you see* I will give *to you* and to your descendants" (13:15). What does Abraham think of the Lord's promise made at Shechem, and how does he regard the land since it is not yet promised to him? He may be wrong in leaving it, but his leaving it may show that he does not yet think of it as "promised land." What is "this land"? Is it all of Canaan as the Lord will make explicit later at Bethel, or is it just Shechem where Abraham is at the time? Abraham is leaving the "Promised Land" as soon as he departs from Shechem for Bethel

(12:8). The text tells us nothing of Abraham's understanding of the Lord's statement, and we are left with a wide range of possible elucidations of Abraham and of each aspect of the narrative that is significant for his characterization.

To return to the commentaries, some note the immorality of Abraham's behavior, especially the deception which ends with Sarah in Pharaoh's house, and draw no moral lesson from it. Vawter considers it secondary as the purpose of the tale is to portray "Abraham as a man of shrewdness and sagacity in his time" and to show that he is "under God's specific and continuous protection." He goes on to say that we must "excuse" the narrative since it works with "an outmoded scale of priorities" (181–82). Koch concludes his similar discussion by noting that "all this points to very early conditions" (127). These are versions of Gunkel's interpretation. Skinner refers to "primitive features of the legend" and states that "the ethical code to which the narrative appealed" did not severely condemn deception or personal cowardice (247). The text, in these expositions, is put aside by relegating parts of it to a secondary, "primitive" status and finding its core, its primary purpose, in a general, univocal assertion.

Indeed, many commentators feel that Genesis itself, particularly Genesis 20, reflects an unease with the morality of 12:10–20. Skinner claims that Genesis 20 was "written from a more advanced ethical standpoint" (315). Von Rad agrees and adds that it was written with "much more consideration [for] . . . a reflective, indeed sensitive, and theologically refined readership" (221). Abraham is not a total liar as Sarah is at least his half-sister, "Besides she is indeed my sister, the daughter of my father but not the daughter of my mother" (20:12). Their assertion that she is his sister was agreed upon long ago when they left Haran: "at every place to which we come, say of me, He is my brother" (20:13). Von Rad is of the opinion that this "seems less offensive . . . than it did in the conversation on the road, with its almost cynical utilitarian consideration (ch 12:11ff)" (222). Vawter comments that

> in this doublet and in the further J doublet of chapter
> 26 . . . it is made clear that while the patriarch's wife's
> virtue had been put in jeopardy it had in fact, providen-
> tially, been preserved from compromise. (181)

The entire line of argument stems from a limited and narrow reading of Genesis 20; a limited reading of the story itself, of its setting in Genesis, and of its relations to the analogous episodes in Genesis 12 and 26. Much is left out. Reasons for my conclusion are found in my foregoing reading of Gen 20:11–13, and they are further buttressed by my succeeding reading of other parts of Genesis 20 and its setting. In short, Abraham is even more reprehensible in Genesis 20, and serious doubt is cast upon the reliability of his statements in Gen 20:11–13.

Genesis 12, 20, and 26:
A Husband, His Wife, and a Third Party

The three texts in Genesis 12:10–20, 20, and 26:1–14 were the subject of a study by Robert Polzin—"'The Ancestress of Israel in Danger' in Danger"—in which he analyzed them in their biblical context and order and did not remove them from the context nor attempt to arrange them in a historical-ethical progression. He argued that the three revolve around the question of who is blessed and how are we to know. Evidence of blessing is sought in the possession of wealth and progeny, both gained in a proper fashion. Thus, in Genesis 12 Abraham gains wealth illegitimately and therefore is not granted progeny. In Genesis 20 he gains wealth legitimately, after the removal of the adulterous situation, and is granted progeny, Isaac, soon afterwards. A sub-theme is the modes of learning God's will which are found in the ways that the king discovers the truth that the patriarch's "sister" is actually his wife. In Genesis 12, the Lord intervenes directly with punishment to instruct Pharaoh; in Genesis 20, God intervenes in a dream to warn Abimelech; in Genesis 26, Abimelech learns through his own observation of Isaac and Rebekah. Polzin related these to the biblical modes of revelation in narrative, God's actions; prophetic literature, dreams and visions; and wisdom literature, human observation and reason.

In a subsequent article, "Literary Unity in Old Testament Narrative," I argued for an extension of Polzin's study to include the Abigail and David and David and Bathsheba stories which are respectively in 1 Samuel 25 and 2 Samuel 11–12. I did this on the basis of a more general view of the characters involved. Instead of a patriarch, his wife, and a foreign king, I focused on the trio: a husband, his wife, and a third party. On the basis of the trio, I developed a series of five narratives that needed to be "explained," and my analysis took the form of a moral treatise. Let me cite a portion of my conclusions:

Such extension resulted in the addition of three important issues to his [Polzin's] conclusions: one, divine revelation must have a physical, manifest aspect discernible by human observation and reason; two, the moral order itself can be regarded as a mode of divine revelation; three, moral sensitivity and responsibility require consideration of the present situation and of the possible results of any action. Also, such consideration must take Yahweh's will into account, however it may have been determined; this is crucial to one who has received direct revelation of God's will. (41)

I focused the analysis on David's sin with Bathsheba and concluded "that only in comparison and contrast with the previous four [stories] can we assess the true extent of David's immorality" (42).

Sharp criticism of both Polzin's and my articles are contained, explicitly and implicitly, in my readings and comments to this point. I do not need to rehearse all of them. In my earlier study, I was compelled to reach some solid conclusions, some explanation of why the series of five texts exists in the OT narrative in the first place. I "forced" the issue by taking one overarching pattern as the pattern and as a definite pattern unmarred by ambiguity or equivocation. There was no talk of a continuum or a spectrum; issues were stated clearly and distinctly. My concern now is tracing the tension and play inherent in such a group of stories, assessing how they affect the reading of any given one. Gen 12:10–20 is my starting point, my initial thread.

The series of stories involving a husband, his wife, and a third party can be extended beyond the five already mentioned: Abraham and Sarah in Genesis 12 and 20; Isaac and Rebekah in Genesis 26; David and Abigail in 1 Samuel 25; and David and Bathsheba in 2 Samuel 11–12. In my earlier article, I stated that the Garden of Eden story in Genesis 2–3 and the Joseph and Potiphar's wife tale in Genesis 39 fit the category. Now I also include the narrative of Ahab, Jezebel, and Naboth in 1 Kings 21 and the brief episode with Moses, Zipporah, and the Lord in Exod 4:24–26 since it does involve the trio of characters and, as in most of the other stories, the theme of murderous violence. There are at least nine narratives in the "paradigm."

For the present, I note the many possibilities for comparison and contrast of the various members based on thematic and word studies, structural parallels and inversions, and each story's relation to its own context. Thematic and word studies include sin and its consequences, whether it is punished or not. Sin entails, among other issues, human desire and its fulfillment, especially by violent means. This relates to life and death which is thematized in most of the narratives. "Blessing" is also shared by most of them. Polzin focused on its importance in the stories in Genesis 12, 20, and 26. In 1 Kings 21 it is present in the enigmatic and probably euphemistic charge against Naboth that he "blessed" God and king (21:10, 13). Among the consequences of sin is a concern for children either as successors or as the ultimate recipients of punishment. God's intervention, both its rationale and its effects, is noteworthy. Structural parallels and inversions serve other studies by noting, for example, the general identity and relationships of the three central characters.

Such studies do not result in the establishment of an "explanation," a single set of themes or a common structure. Attempts to trace words, themes, structures, etc., end in the construction of ever more elaborate networks of analogies. There is no final, last network that definitively accounts for all the narratives.

A common theme in Gen 12:10–20 and 1 Kings 21 is (royal) desire and its fulfillment through murder; the relation between the two texts, however, is complicated. Abraham, the Israelite, incorrectly fears that the Egyptians, the foreigners, will do to him what Jezebel, the Israelite queen and foreign woman, does to Naboth the Jezreelite.

The analysis could be extended, but would not account for both texts since they "branch out" into elaborate networks. The Kings narrative is part of the story of the house of Ahab and its clash with the prophets, especially Elijah, over Baal worship and its ultimate annihilation by Jehu (2 Kings 9–10). The fate of Ahab and his two sons is complicated by the matter of the precise fulfillment of Elijah's prophecy in 1 Kgs 21:19–29. Each chapter and its relation to the Naboth text would have to be assessed; we would be far from the Genesis text with which we started, yet we would not be entirely cut off from it; it would still be part of the reading of the story of the house of Ahab.

Violence, whether murderous violence or the fear or threat of violence, is a theme common to most of the nine stories of the "paradigm." Violence and its relation to royalty is important whether as an instrument of the king or queen to realize their desires or as a scourge that plagues the royal house. For example, David's violence, the murder of Uriah and the taking of Bathsheba, results in Nathan the prophet's proclamation that "the sword shall never depart from your house" (2 Sam 12:10), and it never does. Nathan's denunciation dramatically introduces the theme of progeny: "the child that is born to you shall die" (12:14). Bathsheba then gives birth to Solomon, "And the Lord loved him, and sent a message by Nathan the prophet; so he called his name Jedidiah, because of the Lord" (12:24–25). I leave the texts in abeyance for the time to return to the reading of Genesis 12.

Genesis 12:10: A Famine in the Land

Gen 12:10 introduces the story of Abraham and Sarah in Egypt: "Now there was a famine in the land. So Abram went down to Egypt to sojourn there, for the famine was severe in the land." He goes "to sojourn," not to dwell permanently. A useful study needs to be made of Abraham's modes of living—dwell, sojourn, tent, etc.— and their associations with the places lived in. Ways of interpreting the relation of the descent to the call in 12:1–9 were mentioned before. Is Abraham "sinning" by leaving the promised land, or is this expected, even wise, behavior in the face of a severe famine? Is the question affected by the fact that Abraham "went down to Egypt to sojourn there"? Another famine occurs in Isaac's time "besides the former famine that was in the days of Abraham" (26:1). There is not another explicit reference to the episode of Abraham and Sarah in Egypt, although there is the possible oblique reference quoted and discussed above: "at every place to which we come, say of me, He is my brother" (20:13).

"And Isaac went to Gerar . . . and the Lord appeared to him, and said, 'Do not go down to Egypt; dwell in the land of which I will tell you. Sojourn in this land . . .'" (26:1–3). This is an indirect comment on Abraham's descent into Egypt; Isaac is being singled out for special treatment. Abraham "sins," and he does not "sin." A parallel is not cited as just support or evidence for an interpretation of the text under consideration; this privileges the latter and makes the former a parallel of it whereas they are parallel to each other and to other texts. The effects of similar texts are not one-way, but flow in all directions; the "parallel" text is already the "primary" text and affected by the "parallel" text. A similar example: Isaac cannot return to Haran to obtain a wife for himself (24:3–8), nor can he go down to Egypt to escape famine. Jacob does both for those reasons. This is a negative comment on Jacob's journeys; Isaac is being singled out for special treatment. Jacob errs, and he does not err.

Subsequently Jacob refuses to go to Egypt despite the fact that there is a famine in the land (Genesis 42–45); he goes years later after the revelation of Joseph's existence in Egypt (45:26–46:7). Did Abraham go or should he have gone through an initial refusal to leave Canaan? The parallel with Jacob and the Joseph story indicates why the episode of Abraham and Sarah in Egypt is such a powerful example of the paradigmatic play of OT narrative. I am not concerned just with the text of Gen 12:10–20 in its context and with its relations with the stories in the "paradigm," but wish also to trace any other parallel themes, terms, structure, etc., to construct the network(s) of analogy beginning to form in my reading.

Genesis 12:11–13: Abraham's Proposal

These are Abraham's first recorded words containing his proposal to Sarah and his rationale:

> I know that you are a woman beautiful to behold; and when the Egyptians see you, they will say, "This is his wife"; then they will kill me, but they will let you live. Say you are my sister, that it may go well with me because of you, and that my life may be spared on your account. (12:11–13)

The various parts of the statement are paralleled directly or inversely in the other members of the series. The more obvious themes are: deceit, the beautiful woman (or man), desireability, and a concern with death (murder) and life. Abraham's argument is narrow and truncated. He fears that the Egyptians will kill him, but he does not say why. Nor is it evident what Abraham hopes to gain by passing Sarah off as his sister. He will stand in a better position to protect her as her brother according to Keil-Delitzsch (197), but Abraham says nothing about protecting her. Another "logical" argument is that the Egyptians will see a beautiful woman and murder her husband so that one of them can have her; this assumes that Egyptians are immoral and will commit murder to avoid committing adultery. This is Skinner's argument (248–49), but Abraham says nothing about any presumed immorality of the Egyptians.

"Abraham said, 'I did it because I thought, There is no fear of God at all in this place, and they will kill me because of my wife'" (20:11). Previously I noted the circumstances surrounding the "excuse" by Abraham raise serious doubts about its reliability. That reading of 20:11–13 gains support from 12:11–13. Abraham, in private to Sarah, feels no need to bring any religious dimension into the argument; his statement to Abimelech about "fear of God" reflects the public circumstances and not Abraham's beliefs or motives. Finally, the statement in 20:11–13 is in sharp contrast with Abraham's intercession with God in Genesis 18 when he was able to consider the possibility of the presence of righteous people in the arch-evil cities, Sodom and Gomorrah. Or, should I reverse the effect of the analogy and re-read Genesis 18 in the light of Genesis 20? This would produce a quite different understanding of Abraham and his intercession with God.

Moreover, in Genesis 12 Abraham's expressed concern is for himself; this does not correspond to the implied "logical" argument presented above. He says that the Egyptians will kill him and let Sarah live, not take her as a wife. He mentions nothing of Sarah's fate, particularly the situation she could be in if she masquerades as his sister. The disregard for Sarah, his wife, conforms to Abraham's treatment of both her and Hagar, Sarah's servant and his wife. In Genesis 16, Abraham apparently has not informed Sarah of the Lord's covenant and promises narrated in Genesis 15, and he takes a passive role in the Sarah and Hagar conflict, leaving it to them to resolve their problems: "Your maid is in your power; do to her as you please" (16:6). In Genesis 17, Abraham is expressly told by the Lord that the promised heir will be born to Sarah within one year (17:15–21). In Gen 18:9–15, it is evident that Abraham has again not informed Sarah of such an important and, for her, personal piece of information. In Genesis 20, despite his knowledge that Sarah is to be the mother of his son and heir Isaac, whom she is probably already carrying, Abraham still passes her off as his sister and again exposes her to an adulterous situation.

In Genesis 21, in contrast to the conflict between Sarah and Hagar in Genesis 16, Abraham has a reaction to the tension, but not because of any affection or concern for them. It "was very displeasing to Abraham on account of his son" Ishmael (21:11). In Genesis 22, Abraham says nothing to Sarah of God's command to sacrifice Isaac. Indeed, about the only concern that Abraham shows Sarah is that she is buried in a proper site, and then the concern may be for the proper site and not for a proper burial for Sarah (Genesis 23).

In summary, what can be said is that Abraham, in Gen 12:11–13 and in 20:11–13, and Isaac in 26:6–11 are expressing a fear that residence in a foreign place with their wives will result in their murder. They regard perception of beauty, desire, and murder as connected; the first two necessarily and inevitably lead to the third. But the fear as expressed, whether sincere or not, is not presented rationally or logically; it does not derive from a set of facts and developed argument. The precise relationship between the feared events is not stated. Yet Abraham and Isaac act, or at least claim to act, on the fear; they deceive the kings, and the consequences for their hosts are disastrous or potentially disastrous (12:17, 20:3–18, 26:10–11). In Genesis 12, there is the exact progression: "When Abram entered Egypt the Egyptians saw that the woman was very beautiful. And when the princes of Pharaoh saw her, they praised her to Pharaoh. And the woman was taken into Pharaoh's house" (12:14–15). The murder that Abraham explicitly stated he feared would happen has supposedly been averted by his deception, but the unstated and perhaps unforeseen consequence of Sarah as Pharaoh's wife has occurred.

Themes of perception (of beauty), desire, adultery, and murder marked by an element of illogicality are found in 2 Samuel 11 and 1 Kings 21. David sees a beautiful woman, takes her in adultery, and after having her husband Uriah killed, in marriage. Ahab sees a vineyard which he wants, but Naboth, its owner, will not sell or trade. Jezebel, Ahab's wife, proceeds to have Naboth killed and to give the vineyard to her husband who goes to take possession of it. There is an echo of the Garden of Eden: "When the woman saw that the tree was good for food, and that it was a delight to the eyes, and that the tree was to be desired to make one wise, she took of its fruit and ate; and she also gave some to her husband, and he ate" (Gen 3:6)/4/. The illogical element in the two narratives in 2 Samuel 11 and 1 Kings 21 is why murder. David could have bought off or banished Uriah or dealt with him by some exercise of his royal power/5/. Murder comes quickly to mind as the only solution; the same applies to Jezebel. "Do you not now hold rule in Israel?" Jezebel asks Ahab (1 Kgs 21:7). An expected consequence would be, "therefore, take the vineyard and do not worry about Naboth." But again murder is apparently the only strategy thought of by her. Murder makes less sense in the context since the issue is a vineyard, not adultery and a pregnant woman.

The crimes of David and Ahab both result in a prophetic announcement of divine judgment, judgment which concerns the fate of two sons who are brothers and the longer range fate of the monarch's "house." One son dies because of David's sin, but the brother, Solomon, lives and eventually succeeds David on the throne

(2 Sam 12; 1 Kgs 1–2). There is also the announcement that "the sword shall never depart from your house" (2 Sam 12:10). David's line may go on, but it will always be accompanied by violence. Ahab's "house" is to be annihilated. "I will utterly sweep you away, and will cut off from Ahab every male, bond or free, in Israel" (1 Kgs 21:21). His two sons, Ahaziah and Jehoram, both succeed to the throne, but die untimely deaths. Jehoram and the remainder of the house of Ahab are swept away in Jehu's purge (2 Kings 9–10). It is noteworthy that the announcement of the annihilation of his house does not come because of Baal worship, which is so central to the preceding Ahab and Elijah stories in 1 Kings 16–19.

Jehu's purge is thorough; all of Ahab's possible successors are annihilated. His daughter Athaliah is killed by the Judeans after she ruled in Jerusalem for seven years as a usurper (2 Kings 11:1–16). The analogy between the houses of David and Ahab is extended. When Athaliah heard that her son, Ahaziah of Judah, was dead, "she arose and destroyed all the royal family," except for one. "Jehosheba . . . took Joash the son of Ahaziah, and stole him away from among the king's sons who were about to be slain" (2 Kings 11:1–2). The house of David has one survivor left, and he is a descendant of the house of Ahab: Joash the son of Ahaziah. Ahaziah is the son of Jehoram and Athaliah (see 2 Kgs 8:16–18, 25–26). The house of David is contaminated with the curse of annihilation that has been pronounced on the house of Ahab.

"One survivor left": did this also occur with Solomon after fratricide and war had eliminated many of his brothers? It is not so stated in 1 Kings, but after the mention of other of the king's sons in 1 Kgs 1:9 and 25 and the murder of Adonijah (1 Kgs 2:23–25), no other mention is made of Solomon's brothers. In any case, Solomon goes on to build and dedicate the Jerusalem temple (1 Kings 6–9). Joash, in a pathetic contrast, attempts to repair the temple by gathering donations from the people, but nothing is done for twenty or more years (2 Kgs 12:4–8)/6/. The implication is that the priests appropriated the money for their own use. More donations are collected and repairs made, "but there were not made for the house of the Lord basins of silver, snuffers, bowls, trumpets, or any vessels of gold, or of silver, from the money that was brought into the house of the Lord" (2 Kgs 12:13; contrast 1 Kgs 7:15–50). What little Joash is able to accomplish or maintain from the past is soon wiped out. Hazael of Syria attacks Jerusalem, and Joash takes all the gifts and the gold from temple and palace and gives them to Hazael who then ceases his attack (2 Kgs 12:17–18). Truly, "the sword shall never depart from your house."

In comparison with Genesis 12, the two stories of David and Ahab involve royal power and the possible exercise of it in a violent manner. A king or queen may murder simply because he or she wants something and perhaps has already taken it. Other modes of action may be open, but royal power and desire seem to have a close, if not necessary, relation to violence and murder. This statement, in view of Genesis 12, 20, and 26, should not be expressed so generally, since in those passages the kings do not act violently. It is kings and queens of Judah and Israel for whom murder is an automatic recourse, and it is Hebrews, Abraham and Isaac, who assume that desire and murder are necessarily related/7/.

As it turns out, Abraham's and Isaac's fears of being killed are unfounded, whereas Uriah and Naboth demonstrate no fear in situations where they have every right to fear being killed. David, Ahab, and Jezebel are guilty of murder; they are "sinners." Uriah and Naboth may be innocent; they are not prudent. They apparently pay no heed to possible consequences of frustrating royal desire. Naboth refuses to sell his vineyard to Ahab with an oath, "The Lord forbid that I should give you the inheritance of my fathers" (1 Kgs 21:3). It is not so certain whether this is a serious and legitimate reason for the refusal or whether Naboth is refusing and citing an inconsequential reason made to appear serious by being cast as an oath (Whitelam, 170–81). Uriah may know or at least suspect what David is trying to involve him in and is thus playing with David; if so, it is for ultimate stakes. Both Uriah and Naboth may have a strong complicity in their own deaths.

The Genesis texts, particularly Genesis 20 with its explicit moral statements, gain in view of the David and Ahab narratives. In Genesis, there are fears and threats of death, but no one in fact dies or is killed; life, as the birth of children (Gen 20:17–18), is connected with them. The foreign king is duped. In Genesis 12, he commits adultery and is punished for it, but not killed. In Genesis 20 and 26, the king does not commit adultery because of God's warning or because of the evidence of his own eyes. There is a threat of death because of the adulterous situation, but the threat is averted by returning the woman to her husband (20:3–7; 26:10–11).

Genesis 20 is explicit in the clarification, by the statements of Abimelech, God, and the narration, of Abimelech's moral position and of his possible future actions and their respective consequences.

> Then God said to him in the dream, "Yes, I know that you
> have done this in the integrity of your heart, and it was I
> who kept you from sinning against me; therefore I did not
> let you touch her. Now then restore the man's wife; for he
> is a prophet, and he will pray for you, and you shall live.
> But if you do not restore her, know that you shall surely
> die, you, and all that are yours. (20:6–7)

What is striking in a chapter marked by moral discourse is the absence of a similar clarity in Abraham's moral or religious position; the same lack is found in Genesis 12 and 26. Abimelech accuses Abraham of bringing a great sin upon him and upon his kingdom and of "doing things which should not be done" (20:9). This may describe the events, but it is irrelevant to the narrative. Abraham does not respond to Abimelech's actual questions, and neither God nor the narrative make any comment on Abraham's actions.

Abraham's speeches are crucial to the narrative. His pronouncement of Sarah that "she is my sister" (20:2) sets the plot in motion, and his intercession with God results in the healing that marks Abimelech's justification. "Then Abraham prayed to God; and God healed Abimelech; and also healed his wife and female slaves so that they bore children" (20:17). But it is only the occurrence of these things which is important; nothing is said of their rightness or wrongness. It is the opposite with Abimelech where everything he says and does or that is said of or done to him relates to stating his innocence, "the integrity of his heart."

The imbalance exhibits itself in God's own actions. He punishes Pharaoh, Abimelech, and their houses, and not Abraham or Isaac. Immediately after the encounter with Abimelech, the Lord visits Sarah, and she bears Isaac (21:1–5); after Isaac's encounter with Abimelech, the Lord blesses Isaac with a 100-fold increase in agricultural produce (26:12–14). In all three texts, God's only reference to Abraham or Isaac is in Gen 20:7 where he tells Abimelech that Abraham "is a prophet, and he will pray for you, and you shall live." Abimelech, however, is faced with a threat of death solely because of Abraham's deception. The imbalance is emphasized by the inverted relationship with 2 Samuel 11–12 and 1 Kings 21 where the prophets, Nathan and Elijah, come not to intercede for life, but to pronounce judgment and the death of children.

The parallel texts and the explicit, lengthy statements of Abimelech's innocence combine to focus attention on Abraham's standing; any statements in this regard, as in other aspects of character portrayal, occur on a continuum even though I list them as alternatives. Is Abraham innocent, but fearful; guilty and arrogant; innocent, but ignorant; guilty and fearful, etc.? What does Abraham remember of his experiences in Egypt, and how do the memories affect him? How does he regard the covenants the Lord has made with him; what effect does he think they have on his life, especially what he should and should not do?

Abraham is analogous to Uriah and Naboth since all three stand over against a king and are killed or fear being killed. Uriah and Naboth are naive innocents entangled in affairs that are beyond their abilities to understand or deal with other than to refuse a royal request, or and at the same time, they are sophisticated, perhaps arrogant, men playing a dangerous game with the king by frustrating his plans and desires/8/. Comparisons with Uriah and Naboth, themselves undecidable characters, "prove" nothing, but do construct another part of the network of analogies circulating among the narrative texts.

The preference shown Abraham in Genesis 12 and 20 and Isaac in Genesis 26 is shown David in 2 Samuel 11–12. He is punished by the death of his child, but he himself is spared (2 Sam 12:13–14). Nor is total destruction pronounced upon his house as it is upon Ahab's. One common element is "election." Abraham, Isaac, and David are all called or anointed by God for some purpose that entails the exercise of divine power.

Mention of "election" and divine power brings me to a limit of my present studies, God as a character and force in OT narrative and related issues, e.g., the Elohim-Yahweh distinction and the extent and significance of God's actions and speeches. Thus I put "election" in quotes and do not develop the concept. I do note some of the implications of my readings and make comments on avenues of approach for future studies. The issue of God in biblical narrative is subject to the same tension and play that I have been following in my readings; there is therefore no reason to think that God and issues revolving about him will have any more clarity and definition than other parts of OT narrative.

At present, one topic of interest is the notion of a God who acts in history, a God in control of human events. How is this affected by OT narrative which so often leaves the question of a causal relation between events open? What happens to it when the very conception of "acting in" and "controlling" (causing) becomes clouded and undecidable even on the human level? Can the notion of a God who "acts in history" be maintained in any form?

In their final encounter, Michal rebukes David for dancing before the Ark and thereby exposing himself to the spectators. David forcefully rejects her rebuke. The narrative closes with the comment, "And Michal the daughter of Saul had no child to the day of her death" (2 Sam 6:23). In his analysis of the story, Alter raises the issue of causation in reference to the comment (1978, 62–63). The relation of the statement to the preceding is paratactic; there is no "subordinate conjunction or syntactical signal that would indicate a clear causal connection between the fact stated and the dialogue that precedes it" (63). Alter lists three possible ways of interpreting Michal's barrenness: it is divine punishment for Michal's attack on God's anointed king (see Hertzberg, 281); David has no conjugal relations with her as a personal rebuke for her scathing comments (see Smith, 297); or it is just "a bitter coincidence, the last painful twist of a wronged woman's fate" (Alter, 63). I add that it can be the cause of tension between Michal and David; she has borne him no heir.

Alter states that the biblical authors

> render their protagonists in ways that destabilize any mono-
> lithic system of causation, set off a fluid movement among
> different orders of causation, some of them complementary
> or mutually reinforcing, others even mutually contradictory.
> (1978, 63)

As with his comments on characterization quoted above (18), I agree, and yet at the same time, maintain that the text is putting-into-question the notion of causality/9/. Pursuing the issue of causation, as that of motives and intentions, demonstrates many of the workings of OT narrative, but the concept itself is thereby rendered problematic. If, in relation to another specified event, a given event can be an effect, a cause, or a coincidence, this destabilizes and decenters causation in all its meanings and not just "any monolithic system of causation." In the discussion, Alter does not question the status of the "event" of Michal's childlessness which the OT text itself puts into question: "and the five sons of Michal the daughter of Saul, whom she bore to Adriel the son of Barzillai the Meholath-ite" (2 Sam 21:8).

Mention of God and his actions returns us to the theme of violence, especially murderous violence, which is a major theme in the narratives and part of the shifting play of biblical narrative/10/. It is not a separate, distinct theme, but a thematic scale or range. The Garden of Eden story does not contain the explicit violence of the other members of the "paradigm." There is fear of death in Genesis 12, 20, and 26, but no death in fact. In Genesis 39 the charge of Potiphar's wife against Joseph does include violence, attempted rape, but it is not murderous. Nor is Joseph executed or even threatened with death; he is imprisoned by Potiphar. Again, an Egyptian, a foreigner, acts in a manner quite different from that in which an Israelite would probably act. In Exod 4:24–26, the Lord seeks to kill Moses; murder is not feared or threatened, but actually attempted. Moses, the husband, plays no role. Zipporah, his wife, takes decisive action and averts Moses' death.

David threatens to kill Nabal and his men because of an insult (1 Sam 25:1–22). Nabal's wife, Abigail, is a beautiful woman, but it is not her beauty which is important in the tale of violence; rather it is her "good understanding" (25:3). She convinces David through a persuasive speech not to act on his threat. In Genesis 12, 20, and 26 feared killing did not transpire; here, threatened killing does not take place. Abraham and Isaac hope to avoid the feared death by saying their wives are their sisters; Abigail the wife averts the threatened death. In 2 Samuel 11 and 1 Kings 21, murder is performed for the benefit of an Israelite king, and in each instance a woman is involved. The thread(s) of a woman, her beauty, her role in averting or perpetrating murder, etc., could be followed in the construction of another maze or mazes, but that would take me too far beyond my present goals; I return, therefore, to the theme of violence.

Murderous violence is not to be ascribed only to Israelites, particularly monarchs, since the Lord himself "sought to kill" Moses when Moses was on his way back to Egypt to act on the Lord's command to him (Exod 4:24–26). Indeed, "the Lord smote Nabal; and he died" (1 Sam 25:38). In neither instance does the text provide a rationale for the attempt or the deed. "The Lord smote the child that Uriah's wife bore to David . . . [and] the child died" (2 Sam 12:15, 18). Nathan the prophet has said this happened because of the adultery with Bathsheba and the subsequent murder of Uriah (2 Sam 12:9–12). If this is so, God has violated his own commandment by putting a child to death because of the sin of his father:

> The fathers shall not be put to death for the children, nor
> shall the children be put to death for the fathers; every man

shall be put to death for his own sin. (Deut 24:16; quoted in
2 Kgs 14:5–6)

If this is not the case, then no other rationale is given. In the three
instances in Exodus and 1 and 2 Samuel, the text ascribes specific
acts to the Lord, but they are acts whose significance and
implications are left open.

Genesis 12:13–13:2: Reward and Punishment

"Say you are my sister, that it may go well with me because of
you, and that my life may be spared on your account" (Gen 12:13).
The two reasons are parallel and balanced and connect "it going
well with Abraham" with "his life being spared"; this gives the
impression that the two reasons are the same. Is this so? Abraham
does not say that the deception itself, i.e., the Egyptian's lack of
knowledge that Sarah is his wife, will result in his life, but only that
he will be spared because of her. Does Abraham fear death at the
Egyptians' hands for whatever reason, if any, and is therefore
thinking of bartering for his life with Sarah, "his sister"? If so, does
he have more in mind than just his life? "And for her sake he dealt
well with Abram; and he had sheep, oxen, he-asses, menservants,
maidservants, she-asses, and camels" (12:16). Is Abraham's expressed
fear of the Egyptians sincere or insincere? Perhaps Abraham is
evincing a perverse faith in the Lord's protection, a protection he is
going to use for his material advantage.

"And for her sake he dealt well with Abram." Who dealt well
with him? Pharaoh, the last word in vs. 15, or the Lord, the second
term in vs. 17? "And the Lord afflicted Pharaoh and his house with
great plagues because of Sarai, Abram's wife" (12:17). The Lord's
action and motivation are expressly stated, but what is the effect of
the punishment? The narration does not explicitly relate the affliction to Pharaoh's discovery of the truth, and Pharaoh makes no
mention of punishment or plagues in his rebuke. The parallels in
Genesis 20 and 26 expressly narrate the mode of the monarch's
discovery and lead the reader to assume a causal relation here, but
the text does not support it as the definitive interpretation. The
Lord has acted, but to what effect?

Von Rad assumes that the Lord's affliction was regarded by
Pharaoh as punishment and that he then connected it with Sarah.
Nevertheless, von Rad is aware that the text does not expressly
indicate how Pharaoh made the connection nor does it answer

"other more difficult questions" which von Rad does not even bother to ask. He concludes that

> the story, which began so humanly and understandably, brings us at its end terribly face to face with the darkness and mystery of Yahweh's power, for which no explanation is adequate . . . our determination to understand is limited by Yahweh's power and mystery. The interpreter has to know about this limitation. (163–64)

The text with its bothersome details and lacunae has been definitively interpreted and understood since it teaches that our interpretation is limited, not by a terse and equivocal text, but by "Yahweh's power and mystery." To reiterate, von Rad is assuming that Pharaoh's realization that Sarah is Abraham's wife is an effect of the Lord's afflicting Pharaoh. He interprets the lack of an explicit statement of the causal relation between affliction and knowledge as signifying the Lord's mysterious activity. I, on the contrary, am raising the possibility that Pharaoh's realization is not related to the Lord's afflicting him, i.e., the text is saying nothing about Yahweh's power and mystery. Again, the text supports both readings, von Rad's and mine, but it does not support either as the sole definitive interpretation.

Vawter likewise assumes that Pharaoh perceived the plagues as punishment and connected them with "the presence of Sarah in his harem." He too is aware that the text says nothing about how Pharaoh perceived this or made the association. Vawter, however, does ask another question: "And what revealed to him that she was a wife and not a sister?" He provides a response of sorts:

> The storyteller, singlemindedly devoted to the chronicle of the fathers and not to other issues of logic or even fair play, would doubtless have looked on such questions as frivolous and quite beside the point. (182)

The text is reduced to "the chronicle of the fathers"; this is the core, the essential meaning. Other themes, issues, and such, are not to affect the reading since they are "frivolous and quite beside the point." This is a fine example of a univocal interpretation which expressly rules out other interpretations and any equivocations or problems that accompany the proffered interpretations.

It is also an example of reduction of the text by regarding its details and gaps as part of Hebrew style; "this is simply the way they told their stories." "The way" is not to be investigated or

questioned further for its significance, implications, etc., since they
are already known. "Hebrew style" signifies "Hebrew style."

Pharaoh's rebuke of Abraham is stinging:

> What is this you have done to me? Why did you not tell
> me that she was your wife? Why did you say, "She is my
> sister," so that I took her for my wife? Now then, here is
> your wife, take her, and be gone. (12:18–19)

Abraham does not and perhaps cannot respond; ample material for
conjecture about Abraham's motives and reactions have been provided in the preceding discussions. Pharaoh sends him away "with
all that he had," and Abraham goes up from Egypt with "all that he
had" (12:20–13:1). Pharaoh permits Abraham to keep his gains. He
is happy to be rid of Abraham even if the latter is enriched; he will
not take back what he has given even if the giving was done
because of a deception. Or he, like Abimelech in Genesis 20, is
concerned with Sarah's honor; "it [wealth] is your vindication in the
eyes of all who are with you; and before every one you are righted"
(20:16). Finally, the text notes that "Abram was very rich in cattle,
in silver, and in gold" (13:2). I have noted Polzin's comment on the
status of this wealth; it has been acquired improperly, is not accompanied by the birth of a child, and is therefore not a sign of blessing. The themes of wealth and blessing in Genesis are in need of
further investigation since they go far beyond the limited number
of texts that I have been analyzing.

Genesis 12:10–20: A Mini-Exodus

Abraham's descent into Egypt forms a "mini-Exodus." He
deceives the Egyptians as God and Moses do with the demand, "Let
my people go, that they may hold a feast to me in the wilderness"
(Exod 5:1, et. al.). Moses' commission is to bring the people out of
Egypt and into the Promised Land, not just for a feast in the
wilderness (Exod 3:7–10). Pharaoh and his house are smitten with
plagues in Genesis 12 and in Exodus 7–12. Pharaoh commands
Abraham "to go" (Heb.: hālak) and then "sends him forth" (Heb..:
šālaḥ); in Exodus the same terminology refers to Israel's "going"
(e.g., Exod 3:19; 8:24; 14:29; 15:19) and "going forth" (e.g., Exod
5:1, 2; 7:16; 12:33; 13:17).

The parallel has been perceived and developed in more detail
by Cassuto (334–37), but the analogy does not trouble him since the
object of the story, "like that of all Pentateuchal narratives, is to

instruct its readers" (336). Instruction, teaching, and inculcation are for Cassuto frequently the essence, the true meaning, of biblical narrative. The analogy between the Exodus and Gen 12:10–20 teaches that "the bondage of the children of Israel in Egypt was not an accidental calamity, but part of a plan prepared beforehand" and "that the Lord is ever ready to protect his faithful ones" (337). As with von Rad, the specific biblical text is put aside since it has served its purpose by "teaching us something."

The "mini-Exodus," however, is inverted in terms of "good guys" and "bad guys." The Egyptians are not oppressors in Genesis; they are not "hard-hearted." Indeed, Pharaoh is aware of the moral issues entailed once he learns that Sarah is Abraham's wife. The Egyptians in Genesis are far from the Egyptians in Exodus. Yet Abraham is not so far from Moses and Israel. I have already indicated some of the possibilities for a comparison between Abraham and Moses, and how the comparison forms an integral part of the portrayal of the two as characters.

With Abraham, particularly in regard to Gen 12:10–20, the character situation is complicated and enriched by Abraham's analogy, not with an individual, but with the people Israel since it is the people who despoil the Egyptians and then go up from Egypt. It is the people, in their murmurings and rebellions, who are similar to Abraham and his questionable dealings with the Egyptians. Thus, there is no need to appeal to "folk tradition" or to "typology" to interpret Abraham as signifying both individual and nation; the text has already done it. These are pointers for future reading of Genesis and Exodus; to follow them now would carry me far from my present concerns.

Israel survives the oppression and comes up out of Egypt, not because she deserves it for anything she did, but because of God's "election" of her, because of his covenant made first with Abraham.

> And the people of Israel groaned under their bondage . . .
> and God heard their groaning, and God remembered his
> covenant with Abraham, with Isaac, and with Jacob. And
> God saw the people of Israel, and God knew their condition.
> (Exod 2:23–25)

Abraham's survival and ascent from Egypt are due to his cunning, Pharaoh's reluctance to punish him, the Lord's intervention on Abraham's behalf, and chance since Pharaoh's discovery of the truth was coincidental as was Abimelech's in Genesis 26. The parallel with

Exodus where God's covenant with Israel is stressed as his motivation for coming to their aid leads the reader to assume that a similar situation is in effect in Gen 12:10–20. Pharaoh's punishment and knowledge are connected as cause and effect; "the Lord is ever ready to protect his faithful ones," his elect or chosen ones whether an individual or a whole people. Or I could reverse the effect of the analogy and read the Exodus story in light of Gen 12:10–20 which emphasizes, not God's activity and motivation, but the behavior, immoral and otherwise, of the "elect."

The reversal of Egypt's role in the Genesis 12 story characterizes Egypt and Egyptians throughout the book of Genesis. In Exodus, Egypt is the place of oppression, the "house of slavery," where Israel is crushed with hard labor and individual Israelites are killed. In Genesis, on the contrary, Egypt is a place of life and material prosperity. It provides the patriarchs and their families with food in the face of famine and with other material wealth. The key texts are Gen 12:10–20 and the story of Joseph in Genesis 37–50. I also include Genesis 20 and 26 since the Philistines provide both Abraham and Isaac with wealth or the opportunity for gaining wealth, and the Philistines "came forth from Casluhim," the son of Egypt (Gen 10:13–14). In Genesis, Egypt and her descendants provide sustenance and wealth for the patriarchs and their families. Full investigation of Egypt in Genesis will connect with the similar study of the themes of wealth and blessing since they come together in Noah's curse of Canaan, Egypt's brother, for the sin of their father Ham.

> "Cursed be Canaan; a slave of slaves shall he be to his brothers." He also said, "Blessed be the Lord, the God of Shem, and let Canaan be his slave. God enlarge Japheth, and let him dwell in the tents of Shem." (Gen 9:25–27)

Curse, blessing, and slavery (hard work) come together in one text; for me these are particularly inviting threads to be traced in future readings.

Beneficient Egypt and Egyptians go farther. While in Egypt, Abraham gains a lengthy list of possessions amongst which are maidservants (12:16). In Genesis 16, because she is barren, Sarah offers Abraham her maidservant Hagar who bears him his first son Ishmael. Is Hagar one of the maidservants acquired in Egypt/11/? Ishmael in turn marries an Egyptian through whom he becomes a great nation (Gen 21:21; 25:12–18), partially fulfilling the divine promise to Abraham that he will be "the father of a multitude of nations" (17:4). Not just wealth, but even the fulfillment of divine promises come to Abraham through Egyptians.

The reversal between Genesis and Exodus vis-à-vis Egyptians is in evidence in the Hagar episodes. Sarah, the Israelite, deals harshly with or "oppresses" Hagar, the Egyptian, who subsequently "flees" into the "wilderness" where she encounters the "angel of the Lord" (16:7–14). There are parallels with both Israel and Moses. The Israelites are "oppressed" (Exod 1:11–12), subsequently "flee" (14:5) into the "wilderness" (13:8; 14:3, 11) where the "angel of God" (14:19) goes before them. Moses fears Pharaoh, flees to Midian, and in the wilderness, the angel of the Lord appears to him (2:15–3:2). In the second Hagar episode, Sarah demands that Abraham "cast out" (Heb.: *gāraš*) Hagar (Gen 21:10). Abraham complies and "sends her away" (Heb.: *šalaḥ*); Hagar leaves and wanders in the wilderness (21:14–21). Moses and Aaron go to Pharaoh and demand, "Thus says the Lord, the God of Israel, 'Send my people away, that they may hold a feast to me in the wilderness'" (Exod 5:1, *et. al.*). Eventually, the people are "cast out" of the land of Egypt (6:1; 11:1; 12:39; note the name Gershom [2:22] and its connection with the verb *gāraš*). Again, I have only noted some of the threads to be followed in a reading of Genesis and Exodus; nevertheless, they do demonstrate that any reading of Genesis cannot be simple and limit itself to Genesis.

Gen 12:10–20 is a powerful example of the effects of the paradigmatic possibilities of biblical narrative, of how it overloads a text and frustrates any attempt at clear, univocal reading. The main text under consideration does not give enough to support a final, definitive reading, and at the same time, it provides too much. The parallels, analogies, contrasts, and such, also provide too little or too much. Under the impact of paradigmatic interference, the text explodes in all directions.

NOTES

/1/   For example: Gen 7:9, 16; 8:21; 12:4, 11; 17:23; 18:5; 40:22; 41:13; Exod 1:17; 2:14; 5:13; 10:10; 12:32.

/2/   I take the distinction between mode and voice from Genette, *Figures III*, pp. 183–267. See Scholes, *Structuralism in Literature*, pp. 166–67, for a brief presentation of Genette's view.

/3/   Indeed, the discussion of character is dependent on Nietzsche's notes in *The Will To Power*, especially pp. 261–331, "The Will to Power as Knowledge."

/4/   See Clines, "The Significance of the 'Sons of God' Episode," and Petersen, "Genesis 6:1–4," who both note associations between the texts I am discussing and Gen 6:1–4. These present an intriguing line of comparison.

/5/   See Miscall, "Literary Unity," pp. 40–41 for more detail.

/6/   Solomon installs the Ark (Heb.: 'ărōn) in the temple (1 Kgs 6:19) and refers to it frequently in his prayer of dedication (1 Kings 8). After 1 Kings 8, the term 'ărōn occurs only twice more in 1–2 Kings, in 2 Kings 12:10–11 where it refers, not to the Ark, but to the collection box in the temple.

/7/   The situation is further complicated by Jezebel who is a foreign woman, the daughter of a Sidonian king, and an Israelite queen, the wife of Ahab (1 Kgs 16:31).

/8/   Another network can be constructed here by developing analogies with the wisdom literature which is frequently concerned with proper behavior towards royalty.

/9/   See de Man, *Allegories of Reading*, especially ch. 5, "The Rhetoric of Tropes," which is a close reading of some Nietzschean texts.

/10/   "Violence" is encountered in the reading of almost any narrative section within Genesis–2 Kings and must be a concern of future reading of the corpus.

/11/   Plaut, p. 131, notes an Arabic tradition that Hagar was in fact one of the maidservants provided by Pharaoh.

PART II
1 SAMUEL 16–22

Introduction

The following reading of the beginning of the David narrative continues the same modes of close reading employed in the readings of Genesis, and it plots the same types of workings of OT narrative. But now I am reading the David narrative which is different from the Abraham Cycle, and there will be new illustrations of the play of OT narrative and the lengthier development of some points raised earlier in the first part or in the Introduction. My reading focuses on 1 Samuel 16–22 and ranges throughout Genesis–2 Kings for analogous passages. I begin with the text under consideration in its context and then incorporate material that is parallel in any sense; at times, I take into account the context of a given parallel and even some of its parallels. As in the Genesis readings, this does not produce enough for a definitive reading and, at the same time, too much. I follow the text's threads wherever they may lead, but this does not go to the center of the labyrinth, rather it constructs the maze itself. In the readings, attention is given to the deceptive quality of the literal aspect of biblical narration; detailed and clear narration and description is not always matched by clear meaning and significance.

In regard to David himself as a biblical personage, I restrict myself, with a few exceptions, to the material on him within 1 Samuel 16 through 1 Kings 2 since to go beyond this into the statements on him in the rest of the books of Kings, Psalms, Isaiah, Chronicles, etc., would complicate the readings beyond the scope of this work. Future reading will have to take account of the great variety of material on David in the OT with particular concern for the sharp contrast between the David of the books of Samuel and the David of much of the rest of the OT, the David who walked in the Lord's way, keeping his commandments and his statutes.

The David narrative, which I for now limit to 1 Samuel 16 through 1 Kings 2, is approximately four times longer than the Abraham Cycle and contains far more in plot, characters, characterization, themes, etc. The David story also divides into larger sections. The episodes do not "stand on their own" to the same extent as in the Abraham Cycle since there is a "flowing" narrative with more extensive relations, chronological and otherwise, between many of the individual stories. Because of the greater length, there are more parallels to any selected text from within the David material itself. I will still develop parallels within the overall corpus of Genesis–2 Kings, yet those within the David narrative are more inviting since they do involve the same character or characters. On the other hand, precisely because of the invitation, they are very troublesome if they do not result in clarification, but in added difficulties for the reading. (See above, pp. 1–2, for the restriction to Genesis–2 Kings.)

The chronology of the David narrative is presented in a fashion quite different from the Abraham Cycle. The sign posts for the entire story are few, and the first one is not certain. 2 Sam 5:4–5 informs us that David was thirty years old when he became king of Judah at Hebron (2 Sam 2:1–4, 11) and that he reigned over Judah and then over Judah and Israel for a total of forty years. Thus, 2 Sam 2:1 through 1 Kgs 2:12, David's death, covers a period of forty years.

1 Sam 13:1 provides the first chronological sign post. The Hebrew text is difficult, if not impossible, and the RSV does not even hazard a guess as to the number of years involved. Literally, the text apparently says, "Saul was one year old when he began to reign; and he reigned two years over Israel." Many question the two years as being too short a time for the events of 1 Samuel 10–31, but the figure of two years is possible. However, the statement that Saul was one year old when he became king does not accord with the narrative and therefore casts doubt on the reliability of the second statement that he reigned two years. Therefore, we cannot be certain of the period of time elapsed from 1 Samuel 13 through 1 Samuel 31, Saul's death in battle, nor consequently of the time from David's anointing by Samuel in 1 Samuel 16 to his anointing by the elders of Judah in 2 Samuel 2.

The age of one year old is an issue that relates to the text-critical problems in the David material of which there were few in the Abraham Cycle. The problem is also greater in Samuel because of the existence of the Septuagint translations and some Qumran fragments that frequently present texts that diverge sharply from the Masoretic Hebrew Bible (see McCarter, 5-11). Nevertheless, with the exception of the preceding brief discussion, I will not deal with them in the present work. Incorporation of text-critical issues, particularly variants, into future readings of the David narrative is certainly a goal of mine and not always with the aim of establishing the "best text," but of assessing how two or more versions of a given passage will affect a reading of it or of assessing the effect of the very fact that a given passage is textually troubled. For example, 1 Sam 13:1 and its "one year old" date intrigues me in and of itself and also because the tradition, in Hebrew manuscripts and in translations, is almost devoid of guesses at the age. For the present readings, the issue of variants holds especially true for 1 Samuel 17-18 and the much shorter versions contained in some Greek manuscripts.

Even though the elapsed time of 1 Samuel 16 through 2 Samuel 2 is not certain, there is little reason to "rearrange" the episodes; the narrative sequence, in most instances, appears to correspond to a chronological sequence. Explicit time frames, on the other hand, are provided for some of the separate events. For example, 1 Sam 17:55, 18:1, and 18:6 date events to the day of David's defeat of Goliath while 19:11 relates an episode from the next day. 1 Samuel 20 notes which day of the new moon festival is concerned in the dealings between David, Jonathan, and Saul. Finally, 2 Samuel 13-15 provide explicit note of the length of time entailed from the rape of Tamar to the revolt of Absalom. However, the amount of time elapsed between other adjacent stories is seldom given, and at times generalizing and anticipatory statements by the narration upset the strict chronological order of the narrative. For example, 1 Samuel 18:1-9 narrates some of the events of the day of Goliath's defeat, but vs. 5—"And David went out and was successful wherever Saul sent him; so that Saul set him over the men of war"—is a general statement of the future. Other examples are noted in the readings.

The stories and poems in 2 Samuel 21-24 are more troublesome since it is not certain whether each of them fits chronologically between 1 Samuel 20 and 1 Kings 1 or whether they are an appendix of material that fits into the story of David at various times. For example, when exactly had "the Lord delivered [David] from the hand of all his enemies, and from the hand of Saul" (2 Sam 22:1)?

Since the chronological question is undecidable, my attention is drawn to the fact that the stories and poems are presented here, together and like an appendix, without any explicit or definite indication of their relation, temporal or otherwise, to the rest of the narrative. Gathered in this manner and placed at this point in the David story, the material in 2 Samuel 21–24 raises many intriguing possibilities for reading the David narrative; some of them play an important role in my reading/1/.

1 Samuel 16:
The Lord's Anointed and the King's Musician

1 Samuel 16–17 introduces David, the anointed, the king-to-be. The narration offers a story marked by an ordered plot, memorable characters, clearly stated themes, and a well-delineated setting. It offers reliable and essential knowledge of who David is, of why he is anointed, and of what it means to be anointed. There are even some facts about God and his plans and actions.

Yet the text has already withdrawn its offer in a series of feints and dead ends. Explicit details have undecidable and indeterminate significance. The plot is opened by gaps and it cannot be closed. The characters are elusive and cannot be univocally described at any level. Themes are expressly stated and then emptied of content by undecidability and equivocation. Settings are precisely delineated, but their significance is indeterminate; or the setting may not even be stated.

Many of the feints, the dead ends, and indeterminate aspects are noted in biblical commentaries on 1 Samuel, but their force is contained and controlled by rending the text into different sources, traditions, accounts, etc., and by subjecting the fractured text to univocal interpretations that suppress many of the specifics of the text or that fill in the gaps. Commentaries of a conservative persuasion resort also to univocal interpretations or to rewriting the text, to supplying what is "missing." As in the first part on Genesis, I develop a few examples of such modes of interpretation.

1 Samuel 16 divides into two parts. Vss. 1–13 narrate the anointing of David as king to replace the rejected Saul; vss. 14–23 relate David's introduction into Saul's court as musician and armorbearer. Since 1 Samuel 16 introduces David, is his "call narrative" in a sense, it is surprising that he stays in the background; he does little and says nothing.

The first part of the chapter is better termed a "call narrative" of Samuel since the Lord appears to Samuel with a specific commission: "Fill your horn, and go; I will send you to Jesse the Bethlehemite, for I have provided for myself a king among his sons" (16:1). Reminiscent of Moses in Exodus 3–4, Samuel carries out the commission only after an objection that Saul will kill him if he hears of it; the Lord responds by telling Samuel to say he is going to Bethlehem to offer a sacrifice (16:2–3). The narrative tells more of the relationship between the Lord and his prophet than of the one between the Lord and his king, his anointed. On the other hand, 1 Samuel 3, the first "call narrative" of Samuel, contains only the Lord's message explaining what is to happen to the house of Eli and why, but he is given no charge or commission. In 16:1–13 it is the opposite; Samuel is given a commission, but no message, no explanation. David is to be anointed king, but why David is never even addressed as a question. Nor is the matter of the significance and meaning of king or kingship raised or dealt with here. Samuel says nothing to David when he anoints him.

The previous anointing and election of Saul as king in 1 Samuel 9–10 can be cited as a parallel, but it does not help to clarify the particular problem. There is the ambiguity that the Lord sends Samuel to anoint Saul as "prince" (Heb.: *nāgîd*; 9:16, 10:1) whereas the people have Samuel choose them a "king" (Heb.: *mélek*) by lot (10:17–24). The only positive thing said of the king is that "he shall save my people from the hand of the Philistines" (9:16). This is not immediately fulfilled, but Saul does soon win a decisive victory over the Ammonites (1 Samuel 11). The king is related to military victory over Israel's enemies. On the other hand, 1 Samuel 8; 10:17–25 abound in statements of the negative effects of the rule of a king including widespread conscription to man the armies to win him his victories (8:11–12). Indeed, the Lord himself asserts that the people's request for a king is a rejection of him as their king and not a rejection of Samuel (8:7). Nor does the story of Saul in 1 Samuel 13–15 add much, if anything, to a positive appraisal of the king. Thus the Lord's charge to Samuel to go with his oil to Jesse "for I have provided for myself a king among his sons" is apparently a positive, in contrast to the previous highly negative, view of the king. Yet the text tells us nothing about what this particular king will be, other than anointed at the command of the Lord, and it says nothing of why it is he who is to be anointed.

Jesse the Bethlehemite is introduced in 1 Sam 16:1. He is evidently well known since, in vss. 1 and 18, neither Samuel nor

Saul asks for further identification once his name is mentioned. 16:4–5 raises the possibility that he is an elder since the elders of the city meet Samuel and he tells them to consecrate themselves. The narrative continues immediately, "and he consecrated Jesse and his sons, and invited them to the sacrifice." Three of Jesse's sons are introduced by name—Eliab, Abinadab, and Shammah—and apparently in the order of birth. Jesse has yet four more sons, and there is an eighth, the youngest, out tending the sheep. He is finally named in vs. 13 at the end of the episode: David.

In his charge to Samuel, the Lord informs him that the new king is to be one of Jesse's sons, but does not tell him which one. When Samuel sees Eliab, he immediately concludes that this is the anointed. No basis for the conclusion is stated, but the Lord's response implies that Samuel has judged too quickly on the basis of physical appearance: "Do not look on his appearance or on the height of his stature, because I have rejected him" (16:7). The echo of the story of Saul's rise to kingship supports the implication, and thereby the Lord's statement makes an indirect and negative comment on Saul:

> There was a man of Benjamin whose name was Kish . . .
> and he had a son whose name was Saul, a handsome young
> man. There was not a man among the people of Israel more
> handsome than he; from his shoulders upward he was taller
> than any of the people. (9:1–2; see 10:20–24)

"For the Lord sees not as man sees; man looks into the eyes, but the Lord looks into the heart" (16:7). The closing phrase is generally interpreted as an explanation for the Lord's rejection of Eliab, an explanation which engages the dichotomy of "true inner self" versus external and frequently false appearances: "the Lord does not look upon what is external and visible, but upon what a man is like within" (Hertzberg, 138). But this is to go beyond what the Lord says since he does not state what he sees in the heart, or that what he sees differs from what Samuel sees. Nor is the opposition operative elsewhere in the corpus of Genesis–2 Kings; God does not choose a person because he knows their "true inner self." The statement, "man looks into the eyes, but the Lord looks into the heart," may be accurate theologically, but it is a platitude with little or no relevance to the context. It is a feint of the text, an already withdrawn offer of reliable and significant truth.

I read the statement with Isaiah 55:8: "my thoughts are not

your thoughts, neither are your ways my ways, says the Lord."
God's ways are not human ways, and neither Samuel nor we as
readers are to know why the Lord has rejected Eliab or why he has
chosen David. The Lord's initial statement, "Do not look on his
appearance or on the height of his stature," is not necessarily only a
rebuke of Samuel, but also a command, "Do not even glance at him
for I have rejected him," without an explanation of the rejection. As
a rebuke it could also be for transgressing the Lord's explicit command to "anoint for me him whom I name to you" (16:3). Samuel
correctly states that Jesse's next six sons are not the chosen, waiting
for the Lord's specific assertion, "Arise, anoint him; for this is he"
(16:12).

David is finally anointed at the Lord's command, "and the
Spirit of the Lord came mightily upon David from that day forward" (16:13). The narrative says nothing of what David understands this to mean, how he reacts to it, or even whether he has
perceived that the Spirit has come upon him. When Saul was
anointed king by Samuel, "the Spirit of the Lord came mightily
upon him," and he became "another man" with "another heart"
who then prophesied with the prophets (10:6–10). The Spirit came
upon Saul once more, and he went forth to defeat decisively the
Ammonites, and was again declared king (1 Samuel 11). Previously
the Spirit had similarly come upon Samson who immediately performed feats of strength and destroyed Philistines (Judges 14–16).
Thus I, as reader, expect something similar, something new and
decisive, to happen with David. The story of Saul leads me to
expect that David will soon be king; the story of Samson, that
defeat and destruction of Philistines is soon to occur. If it is "there,"
then why not also "here"?

The latter half of 1 Samuel 16 narrates David's introduction
into Saul's court as a skilled musician whose music soothes Saul
when he is tormented by an evil spirit. "Whenever the spirit from
God was upon Saul, David took the lyre and played it with his
hand; so Saul was refreshed, and was well, and the evil spirit departed from him" (16:23). Although the episode in 16:14–23 apparently
occurs after the anointing of David, this is not stated explicitly, nor
is there any indication of elapsed time between the anointing and
the introduction into the royal court.

David is also the king's armor-bearer. Being a musician and an
armor-bearer does not correspond to the previous experiences of
Samson and Saul when the Spirit of the Lord came upon them.

Neither does the text state unequivocally what David thinks of his new situation. *RSV* translates vs. 21, "and Saul loved him greatly," but the Hebrew text is not so explicit. It reads, "and he loved him greatly," and the "he" could be David. Finally, David is apparently a permanent resident of the court as Saul's musician and armor-bearer: "Saul sent to Jesse, saying, 'Let David remain in my service, for he has found favor in my sight'" (16:22).

1 Samuel 16 leaves room for conjecture about Jesse and his family, particularly David. He has been anointed and the Spirit of the Lord has come upon him, but an explanation as to why David is not given. Nor is any significance stated for the Spirit coming upon David, although previous occurrences of the event lead me to expect a decisive action and David's accession to the throne. I expect clarification of the situation and some reason or reasons why David is the anointed.

1 Samuel 16:7: Appearance and Perception

The Lord's statement to Samuel in 16:7 introduced the theme of appearance and perception. One Hebrew root "to see" (*r'h*) occurs four times—three verbal and one nominal—and another root "to see" (*nbṭ*) occurs once for a total of five references to seeing and appearance in one verse. The theme is reiterated in 16:18 which presents one person's perception of David; there will be others. 16:12 has already presented a physical description of David: "he was ruddy, and had beautiful eyes, and was handsome."

The statement in 16:18 is detailed and concerns David's identity, his character:

> One of the young men answered, "Behold, I have seen a son of Jesse the Bethlehemite, who is skilful in playing, a man of valor, a man of war, prudent in speech, and a man of good presence; and the Lord is with him."

Regardless of what the young man makes of his description of David, whether he somehow knows or believes this of David or whether he is just trying to present him to Saul in the best possible light, the literal text of the speech does offer an initial description of David's identity, a description that the continuing narrative should then confirm and elaborate or disprove. I will read 1 Samuel 17 with close attention to the question of David's identity.

The following comments can be made on the separate phrases of the young man's description of David. "Skilful in playing" is confirmed in 16:23 when David's playing gives Saul relief from the evil Spirit. But 18:10–11 and 19:9–10 raise doubts about, if not deny, David's skill with the lyre as his playing fails, on three separate occasions, to give Saul relief. "A man of valor, a man of war" is part of David's character in 1 Samuel, but is of questionable status in 2 Samuel, particularly from the Bathsheba incident on. And war, however David is associated with it, is characteristic of almost all parts of the David story. "Prudent in speech" introduces a theme of speech ("words") and hearing. I will incorporate the theme, plus the theme of appearance and perception, into my reading of the David and Goliath story which presents visible things and audible words, but does not always furnish an interpretation of how they are to be perceived or heard by characters and by readers. "Man of good presence or of good looks" serves no apparent function in the story of David although there are references to the theme in 16:12 and 17:42, Goliath's first impression of David. "The Lord is with him" is repeated by others and by the narration. It is explicitly related to David's military success and to Saul's fear of him, but no further significance of the phrase is expressly given.

> Saul was afraid of David, because the Lord was with him but had departed from Saul. So Saul removed him from his presence, and made him a commander of a thousand; and he went out and came in before the people. And David had success in all his undertakings; for the Lord was with him. And when Saul saw that he had great success, he stood in awe of him. (18:12–15)

The phrase "the Lord is with him" can be associated with the other questions surrounding David's anointing: Why him? What effect does this have on David?

"Man of good presence": of the individual statements, the phrase apparently has no role, explicit or otherwise, to play in the David narrative. Yet there is a faint echo in it of the "paradigm" of stories involving a husband, his wife, and a third party, several of which include the theme of "good presence, good looks": the Garden of Eden narrative (Gen 3:6), Abraham and Sarah in Egypt (Gen 12:11–14), Isaac and Rebekah in Gerar (Gen 26:7), Joseph and Potiphar's wife (Gen 39:6), Abigail and David (1 Sam 25:3), and David and Bathsheba (2 Sam 11:2). With the possible exception of the Abigail and David incident, good looks and appearances do not lead to success, but to disaster or at least to the threat of disaster. And although Abigail does eventually become David's wife, little more is heard of her or of her son Chileab (2 Sam 3:3); not even their deaths are reported. There is a hint in the phrase "man of good presence" of David's future troubles, a subtle reminder that the Lord being with him is not a permanent or unqualified guarantee of success and prosperity. The echo of the "paradigm" also introduces the theme of violence that marks some of the stories and also the entire story of David, whether he is the recipient of the violence of others, e.g., Saul and Absalom, or the violent man himself.

"The Lord was with Joseph, and he became a successful man" (Gen 39:2). That the Lord is with Joseph is asserted four times in Genesis 39, in vss. 2, 3, 21, and 23, and nowhere else in the Joseph narrative. The blessing and prosperity that flow from Joseph are ascribed to the Lord's work four times in Genesis 39, in vss. 3, 5, and 23; no other mention is made in the Joseph narrative of the Lord's intervention on Joseph's behalf. Joseph succeeds and prospers while Potiphar's servant and while in prison because the Lord is with him and is causing the success and prosperity. Whether the rest of Joseph's success is to be ascribed to the Lord's intervention is left open by the narrative. Perhaps the Lord only gets Joseph "off to a good start" in the events of Genesis 39, and the remainder of his life is left up to Joseph. That the Lord is with Joseph is connected in the chapter with success and prosperity in his dealings with others from a position of authority. Joseph is an excellent leader and administrator with and without the Lord's presence.

Challenges and threats to Joseph's effective leadership come from the personal realm. First is the attempted seduction of Joseph, who is "handsome and good-looking" (39:6), by Potiphar's wife; Joseph resists the sexual advance although he is subsequently imprisoned on a false charge. Second is the ordeal that he puts his brothers through before revealing himself as their brother and allowing them and his father Jacob to come and settle in Egypt. Whatever the motivation for the ordeal, Joseph can continue it only so long before breaking down and telling his brothers who he is (Genesis 42–45). Both phrases, "man of good presence" and "the Lord is with him," contain hints of David's troubled life yet to come. He will not resist the temptation of adultery with a woman who is very beautiful (2 Sam 11:2) which will lead in turn to murder, and the combined offense will climax in the prophetic decree that "the sword shall never depart from your house" (2 Sam 12:10). The sword is the symbol of violence that is to consume the Davidic house, and the violence is not restricted to just the events that occur during David's lifetime. We encountered examples in the previous reading of Genesis 12. Nor can David deal with his family, his sons, and eventually reconcile them to himself and to each other as happens with Joseph and his brothers in Genesis 45 and 50:15–21. The narrative of David's sons is the story of the sword, of murderous violence, as brothers kill brothers/2/.

1 Samuel 17: David (?) and Goliath

1 Sam 17:1–3 marks a sudden shift of scene from the court of Saul in Gibeah of Benjamin to a battlefield in western Judah. No mention is made of how much after the events of 1 Samuel 16 the battle with the Philistines took place. However, the exact geographical location is cited, and there is a clear demarcation, the valley, between the Philistines and Saul and the army of Israel. Goliath, the Philistine champion, is introduced and his armor described in great detail.

> And there came out from the camp of the Philistines a champion named Goliath, of Gath, whose height was six cubits and a span. He had a helmet of bronze on his head, and he was armed with a coat of mail, and the weight of the coat was five thousand shekels of bronze. And he had greaves of bronze upon his legs, and a javelin of bronze slung between his shoulders. And the shaft of his spear was like a weaver's beam, and his spear's head weighed six hundred shekels of iron; and his shield-bearer went before him. (17:4–7)

The detail should be significant since such descriptions are rare in OT narrative. The description is associated with the theme of appearance and perception; I will return to it.

Goliath defies and challenges the ranks of Israel,

> Why have you come out to draw up for battle? Am I not a Philistine, and are you not servants of Saul? Choose a man for yourselves, and let him come down to me. If he is able to fight with me and kill me, then we will be your servants; but if I prevail against him and kill him, then you shall be our servants and serve us. (17:8–9)

Saul and all Israel hear him and are "dismayed and greatly afraid" (17:11). Their fear is because they have heard "these words of the Philistine," not because they have seen him; this is noteworthy in view of the description just given of him. And the theme of speech and hearing is brought into prominence. Their fear prevents them from sending forth a champion of their own, but not from fighting with the Philistines (see 17:19-21).

17:12 introduces David by name and then momentarily shunts him aside to present in condensed and explicit form information about his family that was presented in scattered and implicit form in 1 Samuel 16.

> And David was the son of an Ephrathite of Bethlehem in Judah, named Jesse, who had eight sons. In the days of Saul, the man was an elder and distinguished among men. The three eldest sons of Jesse had followed Saul to the battle; and the names of his three sons who went to the battle were Eliab the first-born, and next to him Abinadab, and the third Shammah. David was the youngest; the three eldest followed Saul. (17:12-14)/3/

The apparent situation at the close of 1 Samuel 16 is now clarified and corrected as David divides his time between Bethlehem and wherever Saul is: "David went back and forth from Saul to feed his father's sheep at Bethlehem" (17:15). This state of affairs will soon be definitively ended when Saul will keep David at court and not let him return to Jesse or Jesse's house (18:2).

David's coming and going is paralleled by Goliath: "For forty days the Philistine came forward and took his stand, morning and evening" (17:16). The parallel connects David with Goliath, a connection that will be developed from 17:23 on, but first the narrative provides the tale of how David came to be at the battlefield. Jesse sent him there to see how his brothers were doing.

> And Jesse said to David his son, "Take for your brothers an ephah of this parched grain, and these ten loaves, and carry them quickly to the camp of your brothers; also take these ten cheeses to the commander of their thousand. See how your brothers fare, and bring some token from them." (17:17-18)

David goes the very next morning "as Jesse had commanded him." The previous discussion of Gen 12:4 is pertinent (pp. 12-13); does the "as" signal motivation or a "verbal simile"? David arrives at "the encampment as the army was going forth to the battle line, shouting the war cry. And Israel and the Philistines drew up for battle, army against army" (17:20-21). To this point the narrative is marked by detail and apparent clarity. Much of what was left to conjecture in 1 Samuel 16 has been clarified, and the battle scene leads us to expect that David will soon win a decisive victory.

There are some sections of the narrative, nevertheless, which I wish to isolate since they do raise questions in my mind, questions about the clarity of the narrative to this point when David has arrived at the battlefield and greeted his brothers. First are the detailed descriptions of the battlefield (17:1–3), of Goliath and his armor (17:4–7), and of David's family (17:12–15). What is their significance for the narrative? The first can be taken as a matter of fact, as an "effet de réel," as an offer of objective truth (Barthes, 1968). To this stage of the story, the description of Goliath has served no function other than to be connected with the theme of appearance and perception. It can also be read as factual and objective. 17:12–15 clarifies some points, but it tells nothing new about David; his identity and the significance of his anointing are not touched upon. The description of the family is a feint; its explicit detail provides something solid, but also the empty hope for more.

Through vs. 15, David has been identified three times as Jesse's son. Jesse is concerned with food, particularly as it relates to the proper mode of dealing with the king or some other leader; the concern is obvious in the above quote of 17:17–18, his instructions to David. The same is evident when he first sends David to Saul: "Jesse took an ass laden with bread, and a skin of wine and a kid, and sent them by David his son to Saul" (16:20). He is also an elder (17:12). But such information has no bearing upon the character of David, especially as the newly anointed of the Lord.

Second are the notices, in vss. 20 and 22, that David "has left" first the sheep and then the baggage with "the keepers." The detail can be a mark of David's concern for property, but it can also be other since the verb "to leave" (Heb.: nātaš) has the meaning of "to abandon," "to forsake." David is not just leaving, but also abandoning the sheep and the baggage. A hint of David's character is marked by undecidability, by a continuum and not by a set of distinct alternatives.

"The Philistine of Gath, Goliath by name, came up out of the ranks of the Philistines, and spoke the same words as before. And David heard" (17:23). In contrast to Saul and all Israel who heard and "were dismayed and greatly afraid," no mention is made of David's reaction to what he has heard. This is a striking example of the "there, but not here" effect of OT narrative. The precision and detail of the previous section (17:11) draws attention to the lack of such information in the present section (17:23). The lack of comment on David's reaction also marks a change in the mode of narration since there will now be room to wonder what is happening, what is being said.

> All the men of Israel, when they saw the man, fled from him, and were much afraid. And the men of Israel said, "Have you seen this man who has come up? Surely he has come up to defy Israel." (17:24-25)

Vs. 24 reintroduces the theme of appearance and perception and relates it to the theme of speech and hearing. The imbrication of the themes is marked by the syntax and terminology of vss. 23-25. Vss. 23-25 move from David's talking to the appearance of Goliath who speaks and whom David hears. The men of Israel then see Goliath and flee. Vs. 25 joins the two themes as the men ask about "seeing" the man who has come up to challenge them in a "speech."

All the men of Israel see Goliath, flee, and are very much afraid. The army reacts with fear to both hearing and seeing Goliath/4/. Saul has dropped from the narrative; of him it has only been said that he reacts in fear to hearing Goliath's challenge. Now a function of the description of Goliath in vss. 4-7 can be discerned. Goliath, as described, is seen by the army, and by most commentators, as a formidable warrior who is "perfectly terrifying in his sheer, malevolent power" (McCarter, 295) and who is dressed in "frightening array" (Hertzberg, 149).

But is this the only way to perceive him? Could not he also be seen as a big man encumbered by heavy armor with little range in combat and vulnerable to an attack launched from a distance? His coat of mail weighs 125 or more pounds, he has no bow and arrows, and his shield is carried before him by another, "and his shield-bearer went before him." And, regardless of the reader's view of Goliath, could not this be David's perception of him? The view would be in accord with his determination to fight the Philistine. The remainder of the story does not contradict the assumption; on the other hand, neither does it confirm it as the only possible interpretation. The text never speaks of David seeing Goliath, although it does present Goliath's perception of him: "And when the Philistine looked, and saw David, he disdained him; for he was but a youth, ruddy and comely in appearance" (17:42). The presence of the comment emphasizes the lack of any mention of David's view of Goliath.

The description of Goliath introduces an indeterminate aspect into the narrative through its literal and precise details. They are definite; it is their significance for the narrative, the perception of them by a character or reader, that is equivocal. By playing upon the reciprocity of detail and equivocation, the narrative remains undecidable. With one hand it offers answers to the questions that it raises, but it has already taken them back with the other hand.

The reader's perception of the characters encounters the indeterminability, and the reader is thereby involved in the narrative and its undecidability. The reader is not at a privileged site from which she can perceive "the truth" that lies behind the "appearances": there are visible things presented, but the perceptions of them by others including the reader are not always given. In regard to Goliath, Saul and the army's view of him are stated, but how he is viewed by David or the reader is not stated. Nor does the reader's view have to coincide with that of David, i.e., the reader needs to have perceptions of Goliath, of David, and of David's perception of Goliath. Yet, as just noted, commentaries generally assert the view of Saul and the army as the correct one and the only one for the reader and for all the characters.

However, if I do not know how David sees and reacts to Goliath, than I cannot be sure what I see when David meets with Saul or when he goes out to fight Goliath. The issue is undecidable since I, as reader, do not have the "true perception" of Goliath. My view and David's are both on a continuum that goes from a formidable, frightening warrior to a "sitting duck," and my perception of David and of the combat with Goliath is dependent on the relation of the placement of the two views on the continuum, not to mention that my perception of David himself before the battle with Goliath is already on a scale and does not correspond to a definite portrayal.

The issue is undecidable because it is not the case that Goliath is either a formidable warrior or a sitting duck and that I as reader have to choose and then "prove" one as the only interpretation or as the most probable one. Rather, Goliath is already and at the same time a formidable warrior, a sitting duck, and anything in between. Any given view of Goliath is already upset, destabilized by another view. A continuum is not represented by separate, distinct points, but by an unbroken line on which any posited point slides imperceptibly and inevitably into another point, into the line. And it is not a question of just one continuum, of who Goliath is, but also a question of who David and Saul are, of how they view each other and Goliath, and of what the relationship between them is.

The undecidability of perception, once introduced, thus spreads to other characters to include both their perception of people and things and the reader's perception of them. And since the theme has been linked to that of speech and hearing, it is not surprising to find the same problematic association with hearing. From 17:25 on, despite and because of the great detail, the narrative is marked by undecidability in hearing and perception. It is a matter, although indeterminate, of exactly what a character, or the reader, is seeing and hearing.

17:25–30 is composed of seven quoted or reported speeches. First is the above cited statement by the men of Israel that begins with the reference to the "seeing" of vs. 24 and to Goliath's initial challenge and then asserts that there is to be a threefold reward for the man who kills the Philistine: "and the man who kills him, the king will enrich with great riches, and will give him his daughter, and make his father's house free in Israel" (17:25).

David then asks, "What shall be done for the man who kills this Philistine, and takes away the reproach from Israel?" For the first time in the narrative, the conflict is placed in a religious framework: "For who is this uncircumcised Philistine, that he should defy the armies of the living God?" (17:26). The people respond, "So shall it be done to the man who kills him" (17:27), referring back to the reward just mentioned. This could be an exact quote; the "so" is not shorthand; the content of vs. 25—the threefold reward—has not been literally repeated. Or, the "so" is shorthand; the content of vs. 25 has been literally repeated.

There are different ways of interpreting the exchange. David has heard the statement of the threefold reward, and his question is seeking confirmation of what he has heard. David has not heard the statement, and his question is about some possible reward. In either instance, it is a sincere, literal question. Or, whether or not he has heard the statement in vs. 25, David's question is rhetorical and is directed towards the killing of Goliath, not a subsequent reward. In any case, the people's response assumes knowledge of the preceding assertion of a reward, and it takes no cognizance of the rest of David's speech beyond the question of a reward. They ignore it; perhaps they have heard empty bravado.

Eliab, David's eldest brother, comes on the scene.

> And Eliab his eldest brother heard when he spoke to the
> men; and Eliab's anger was kindled against David, and he

said, "Why have you come down? And with whom have
you left those few sheep in the wilderness? I know your
presumption, and the evil of your heart; for you have come
down to see the battle." (17:28)

He asks David two questions, charges him with evil, and rounding
off his speech, he answers his first question. The content of his
rebuke, however, does not refer to the specifics of David's questions,
but to the fact that David is present and dares to say anything at
all.

David, in kind, responds to Eliab's anger and general rebuke
rather than to the specifics of the rebuke, and the response indicates
that David regards the rebuke as stemming from Eliab's having
heard his previous questions. He has ready answers to Eliab's questions from the narrative; Jesse sent him to see how his brothers
fared, and he "left the sheep with a keeper" (17:17–20). David's two
brief questions—"What have I done now? Was it not but a
word?"—understood as rhetorical questions, lessen the import of his
previous questions by asserting that they were but a word and that
he has done nothing. Or, we can take David's questions as sincere,
literal questions and then answer that he has done much and no,
this was not but a word.

David's first recorded words are questions whose status is uncertain. They are rhetorical questions, i.e., not questions, but the denial
of a question since they assert a literal meaning. For example,
"I did not do anything! This was only a word, nothing more!" Or
and at the same time, they are grammatical and literal questions
asking for specific answers. For example, "What, specifically, have I
done that you are rebuking me? My question wasn't important, was
it?" But it is impossible to decide which interpretation should be
accepted, and this entails unsettling consequences for the entire
reading. Many of David's future "questions" will be marked by the
same problematic and will similarly destabilize the reading/5/.

David turns, asks his "questions" again, and is answered as
before. "And he turned away from him [Eliab] toward another, and
spoke in the same way; and the people answered him again as
before" (17:30). But is this the "before" of vs. 27 or vs. 25? How
many times has David heard the promised reward, if he has heard
of it at all? And if he has heard the specific statement recorded in
vs. 25, what does he make of it? What has he heard, a royal promise or wishful thinking?

This is not a very productive line of approach, but it is one required by the text. Of the seven speeches in these verses, five are directly concerned with the issue of a reward for the man who kills the Philistine, and a sixth concerns it indirectly as, in vs. 29, David apparently depreciates the significance of his foregoing "question." It is to be expected that the reward will be focused on in the remainder of the narrative, that the narrative will clarify the clouded status of the "questions" and "answers," but after 17:30 reward is not mentioned again. David receives no reward or even praise for killing Goliath. Saul does not mention a promise of a reward, although he should know of such a promise. "When the words which David spoke were heard, they repeated them before Saul" (17:31). The importance of "the words which David spoke" is marked syntactically by the use of passive and impersonal verbs; there is no specific subject who hears and then repeats the words. Yet no one makes anything of the words. Saul sends for David immediately after hearing "the words which David spoke," but David speaks first, "Your servant will go and fight with this Philistine." Saul responds to the announcement, "You are not able to go against this Philistine to fight with him," and says nothing about David's "words" which have been repeated to him. David repeats the final part of his previous statement (vs. 26), "this uncircumcised Philistine shall be like one of them, seeing he has defied the armies of the living God" (vs. 36), but makes no reference to any reward.

There are two other possible references to a royal reward, but neither confirms that a reward was ever promised by Saul nor, on the other hand, do they disprove it. The first, in 17:55–58, will be dealt with later. The second is Saul's presentation of his eldest daughter Merab and then of his youngest Michal as wife for David in 18:17–19 and 18:20–27, but the offers stand in ironic relation to the promise of 17:25. Merab and Michal are presented, not because David has killed a Philistine, but so that David may be killed by a Philistine: "Let me give her [Michal] to him, that she may be a snare for him, and that the hand of the Philistines may be against him" (18:21). If the theme of reward, so prominent in the speeches in 17:24–30, is not developed in the narrative, perhaps some other element is developed and can serve as a key to understanding the speeches.

Two of the speeches contain elements that can be detached from the theme of reward. First is David's speech, "What shall be done for the man who kills this Philistine, and takes away *the reproach* from Israel? For who is this uncircumcised Philistine, that he should *defy* the armies of the living God?" "Reproach" and "defy" have the same Hebrew root, *ḥrp*, which is significant since its verbal form occurs also in vss. 10, 25, and 45 where it is translated "to defy" in the RSV. Further, the nominal form occurs in an earlier incident. Nahash the Ammonite asserts that he will "put disgrace [reproach] upon all Israel" (1 Sam 11:2). Saul's subsequent decisive victory over the Ammonites and his reproclamation as king lead me to expect something similar here, especially since, after the victory, Saul declares that "today the Lord has wrought deliverance [victory] in Israel" (11:13). David's second question in vs. 26 accords with the expectation as it speaks of defying or challenging "the armies of the living God," and the theme of divine victory is intoned in David's pronouncements to Saul in 17:36–37 and to Goliath in 17:45–47.

Yet, once spoken by David, the theme of removing reproach and the related theme of divine victory are dropped. Neither the duel with Goliath nor the subsequent rout of the Philistines is described by the narration or by a character as "a victory wrought by the Lord." In a later speech to Saul, Jonathan will so describe David's killing of the Philistine, but it is not certain, in that context, that Saul agrees with Jonathan, nor is the status of Jonathan's speech sure (1 Sam 19:5). I will read the speech in its context when I treat 1 Samuel 19. Finally, the rout of the Philistines (17:51–53) is not a decisive victory as David and Saul's army will soon be engaging the Philistines in continued battle.

A second possible element is the last half of Eliab's speech: "I know your presumption, and the evil of your heart; for you have come down to see the battle" (17:28). The statement adds a third theme, knowledge, to those of perception and hearing; the three are interrelated as perception and hearing should lead to knowledge. Eliab asserts not what he has seen or heard, but what he knows, and his knowledge is far-reaching. He knows David's presumption, or arrogance, and the evil of his heart. Given the Lord's foregoing statement, "man looks into the eyes, but the Lord looks into the heart" (16:7), the latter may be a claim by Eliab to knowledge that is beyond human capacity, i.e., Eliab knows too much. At the end of his grand proclamation to the Philistine, David claims that universal knowledge will result from the defeat of Goliath and the Philistines; "that all the earth may know that there is a God in Israel" (17:46). The narration makes no further comment on the claim.

In the chapter's closing scene, Abner swears to ignorance of David's paternity, "As you live, O king, I do not know," in a situation where, as the army commander, he should know, i.e., Abner knows too little (17:55). The theme of knowledge does not take us any further toward a definitive interpretation than the themes of perception and hearing; nevertheless, we should now also attend to the question of what we do know as readers.

Eliab's statement introduces arrogance and evil and associates them with David; this is an association that will not be broken. Is this how I, as reader, am to perceive, hear, and know David? He is a proud and arrogant man who speaks boastfully to the army, to Saul, and to Goliath with a confidence based on his ability in combat, as evidenced in his past exploits against lions and bears (17:34–37), and on his present realization that Goliath is an easy target for his sling. David is not encumbered with armor and can avoid the spear thrown by the Philistine; moreover, he will have five shots at the Philistine; "[he] chose five smooth stones from the brook" (17:40). Or, according to a slightly different scenario, he is approaching the Philistine in great fear, but with a willingness to gamble his life on the great gains that he can achieve by killing Goliath. David is arrogant and confident of victory; David is arrogant and fearful, but a gambler.

His arrogance and confidence include designs on the kingship. He has been anointed by the venerable Samuel and, being present at the royal court as musician and armor-bearer, has seen first hand Saul's instability. He knows what military victory did for Saul and believes that defeat of Goliath will make him a royal son-in-law. He left sheep and baggage with a keeper because he did not plan to return, i.e., he "abandoned" them. However, he is known and understood by Eliab.

No, Eliab is wrong. David is the pious and innocent young shepherd so familiar in other readings of the chapter, the youth who is deeply shocked by the challenge to God himself that is posed by the Philistine and by the action of the Israelite army. David's statements to army, king, and Philistine are sincere statements of his shock and of his confidence in the power of the Lord and, perhaps, in his own ability. A pious David can have the same perceptions of Goliath as an arrogant David; he can be approaching the Philistine in confidence or in fear.

I could continue to describe possible portrayals of David, to play upon the great number of combinations of the above and other elements, e.g., David's view of Goliath, his religious convictions and statements, his opinion of himself, the accuracy of Eliab's knowledge, etc. This is a fascinating game, but it is a game without conclusion or resolution.

In 17:31–33, David comes before Saul and makes the first of a series of four statements that end with his grand proclamation to Goliath. The first assertion is brief: "Let no man's heart fail because of him; your servant will go and fight with this Philistine." There is no "I," and David personally remains in the background. Saul responds emphatically, "You are not able to go . . . to fight with him for you are but *a youth,* and he has been a man of war from his youth." David refers to himself as "your servant" (Heb.: *ébed),* but Saul calls him "a youth" (Heb.: *ná'ar)* which can also mean servant, but a servant who is a youth, a young man/6/.

Equivocation spreads to the perception of Saul and the hearing of his words. How does he perceive David? How is the reader to perceive Saul? In this central exchange between Saul and David, the narrative says nothing of Saul's thoughts and feelings which have been provided before and which will be provided again. Is Saul expressing an earnest concern for his young musician and armor-bearer, or does he already sense a threat from David, deliberate or otherwise? He is convinced by David's assertions and sends him forth with hope that David will kill Goliath; he is sending him forth, as he will later in regard to Merab and Michal, with hope that the Philistine will kill him. We can play with possible combinations of what Saul sees and hears and of what we see and hear, but the game is unending, undecidable.

David's response to Saul, his second statement, is comprised of two parts. In the first part, David relates his past feats in which he killed lions and bears; he begins with "your servant" and only then shifts finally to "I" (17:34–35). He then draws the relevant point in vs. 36 and reintroduces the religious context. "Your servant has killed both lions and bears; and this uncircumcised Philistine shall be like one of them, seeing he has defied the armies of the living God."

In the second half of the speech, David ascribes the outcome of the past and future conflicts to the Lord's intervention on his behalf; he puts himself farther into the background. "The Lord who delivered me from the paw of the lion and from the paw of the bear, will deliver me from the hand of this Philistine" (17:37). The challenge to Goliath is explicit, and any challenge to Saul is veiled by the form of the speech.

These are the words of a man prudent in speech. The phrase $n^e b\hat{o}n$ $d\bar{a}b\bar{a}r$ in Hebrew has been interpreted as meaning that David is an effective speaker, i.e., his speeches are wise, accurate, and beneficial (Rose, 63–65). It can also be taken in an ironic sense, i.e., David knows well the public and political impact of speech and therefore chooses his words carefully, wisely, for maximum public and political benefit. His speeches are wise, accurate, and beneficial, but for himself and not necessarily for others or for the nation. Yet, as with David's "questions," the status of the phrase, prudent in speech, is indeterminate; it accords, at the same time, with both Rose's and the ironic interpretation. I am not proposing to "determine" its significance as a negative comment on David's speaking ability.

> And David said, "The Lord . . . will deliver me from the hand of this Philistine." And Saul said to David, "Go, and the Lord be with you!" Then Saul clothed David with his armor; he put a helmet of bronze on his head, and clothed him with a coat of mail. And David girded his sword over his armor, and he tried in vain to go, for he was not used to them. Then David said to Saul, "I cannot go with these; for I am not used to them." And David put them off. (17:37–39)

It is not stated whether David is not used to armor in general or just to Saul's armor. David next takes his staff in hand, chooses five smooth stones which he puts (hides?) in his shepherd's bag. "And his sling was in his hand" (17:40); not, "and he took, or chose, a sling." David and the Philistine approach each other; the latter has "his shield-bearer in front of him" (17:41).

The Philistine "looks, sees, disdains" David since he perceives "but a youth, ruddy and comely in appearance"; three times the text uses terms of perception: "looks," "sees," and "appearance" (17:42). This emphasizes that nothing is said of David's perception of Goliath. The latter speaks first, "Am I a dog, that you come to me with sticks?" (vs. 43). "Sticks" is the same word as used previously for David's "staff." Goliath makes no mention of David's sling—an effective weapon—or has David hidden his sling as he did the stones? Both his staff and his sling are "in his hand"; is the staff disguising the sling? Goliath sees "but a youth" when he looks at David. What do we see? What do we perceive when we see this trio—including the shield-bearer—in combat?

Goliath curses David "by his gods" and challenges him, "Come

to me, and I will give your flesh to the birds of the air and to the
beasts of the field" (vs. 44).

> Then David said to the Philistine, "You come to me with a
> sword and with a spear and with a javelin; but I come to
> you in the name of the Lord of hosts, the God of the armies
> of Israel, whom you have defied. This day the Lord will
> deliver you into my hand, and I will strike you down, and
> cut off your head; and I will give the dead bodies of the
> host of the Philistines this day to the birds of the air and to
> the wild beasts of the earth; that all the earth may know
> that there is a God in Israel, and that all this assembly may
> know that the Lord saves not with sword and spear; for the
> battle is the Lord's and he will give you into our hand."
> (17:45–47)

Goliath had cursed David "by his gods," but David names his
God and repeats the charge that Goliath has defied this God himself. His assertion that he will slay the Philistines and feed them to
the birds and the beasts is similar to Goliath's challenge. David's
speech is couched in heavily religious terms, and he portrays himself as the instrument of the Lord of hosts who "saves not with
sword and spear" (see Knierem, esp. pp. 35–36).

This is a dramatic confession of the power of the Lord, of his
concern with and intervention in the course of human history, and
of the conviction that all will come to know him and his power. But
is this a sincere or a self-serving speech by David? What do the
others hear, especially Saul and the assembled army? What do I, as
reader, hear? Regardless of whether David is sincere or not, I am
still confronted with the text of his proclamation. Is it true? Is it
supported by the rest of the narrative? David may be insincere, but
he could be saying more than he knows. However, the battle is not
later described by the Lord or by the narration as a "victory
wrought by the Lord," nor does it result in "all the earth [knowing]
that there is a God in Israel."

"That all this assembly may know that the Lord saves not with
sword and spear." This is a more specific and limited assertion than
the preceding claim for universal knowledge. And even if, in this
more limited instance, "all this assembly" does not acquire knowledge of the Lord's salvation, at least the reader might.

The actual duel between David and Goliath is narrated briefly.
"When the Philistine arose and drew near to meet David, David ran

quickly toward the battle line to meet the Philistine" (17:48). Is this an impetuous move on David's part, a move motivated by fear or confidence in the Lord, or is it an attempt to outflank the shield-bearer and get off a shot before Goliath knows what is happening? What do we see as David and Goliath approach each other, and as David finally kills the Philistine?

> So David prevailed over the Philistine with a sling and with a stone, and struck the Philistine, and killed him; there was no sword in the hand of David. (17:50)

This is an unequivocal statement of the event and evidence that "the Lord saves not with sword and spear."

> Then David ran and stood over the Philistine, and took his sword and drew it out of its sheath, and killed him, and cut off his head with it. (17:51)

This is an unequivocal statement of the event and evidence that "David kills with the sword"/7/.

After all that we have seen and heard, what do we know? Perhaps that the Lord saves not with sword and spear, and that David kills with the sword. The first part is not supported by the rest of OT narrative. At least we know that David has killed Goliath whether with stone or sword, but even this is not certain: "and Elhanan the son of Jaareoregim, the Bethlehemite, slew Goliath the Gittite, the shaft of whose spear was like a weaver's beam" (2 Sam 21:19). (The latter phrase describing the spear occurs also in 1 Sam 17:7.) Now what do we know? This is not the only time that an incident from 2 Samuel 21-24 upsets and complicates the reading of 1 Samuel 17-22.

It is the Philistines' turn to see and flee (see 17:24), but their flight is matched by a bloody pursuit by the men of Israel and Judah who return from the chase and plunder the Philistine camp (17:51–53). The episode is like a patch of blue in the midst of a cloudy, troubled sky.

"And David took the head of the Philistine and brought it to Jerusalem" (17:54). This is an apparent anticipation of the narrative since David's conquest of Jerusalem and his establishment of it as his royal city occurs years later (2 Samuel 5–6; see Willis, 302–4). Whether the verse is an anticipation or not, Jerusalem itself is marked by equivocation in some of the previous biblical books. It belongs exclusively to both Judah and Benjamin, the respective tribes of David and Saul (Josh 15:8 and 18:28). It has not been conquered by either Judah or Benjamin, and the Jebusites, the inhabitants of Jerusalem, live with both the Judeans and the Benjaminites, "to this day" (Josh 15:63 and Judg 1:21). Yet it has been sacked and burned, if not conquered, by Judah (Judg 1:8). Future reading of the David story, indeed of Genesis–2 Kings, will have to take the equivocation into account.

"He put his armor in his tent" (17:54). Whose tent: David's, Goliath's, or someone else's? "Armor" here is the same term as "the things" which David left with the keeper in 17:22, but the verb employed here is different. "To put" does not also mean "to abandon" so this does not have to be a permanent deposit. And apparently it is not since the sword of Goliath will later be located at the sanctuary of Nob (21:9–10).

The final section of the chapter is comprised of two scenes which are marked by precise detail, and yet the final section is opaque, its significance is indeterminable. In the first scene, vss. 55–56, there are two characters, Saul and Abner, while in the second, there are three, David, Abner, and Saul, and perhaps a fourth, Jonathan.

Saul "sees" David going to meet the Philistine and says to Abner, the commander of the army, "Whose son is the youth, Abner?" There are reminiscences in the term "youth" of Goliath's perception of David and of Saul's attempt to dissuade him from fighting, and an allusion in the phrase "whose son?" to the third part of the royal reward: "and make his father's house free in Israel" (17:25). Yet the latter is neither mentioned nor acted upon by Saul. Abner responds formally, "As you live, O king, I do not know!" I have commented on Abner's lack of knowledge. In turn Saul orders him, "Ask, you yourself, whose son the stripling is."

What has happened here? What has been said? What exactly is Saul asking? He should know who David is and whose son he is. Perhaps he is only now beginning to realize that "the youth" who is fighting Goliath is his musician and armor-bearer, the son of Jesse. His question would then mean, "Is this youth truly the son of Jesse, my musician?" Or is it an implied rebuke of Abner for not knowing whose son David is and, perhaps, for not fighting Goliath himself? Where has Abner been during the events of 1 Samuel 17? Later he again has problems recognizing David and is rebuked by David for not keeping a close enough watch over Saul: "Why then have you not kept watch over your lord the king? For one of the people came in to destroy the king your lord" (1 Sam 26:15). And why is Saul's concern with whose son David is and not with who David is? The text, regardless of the status and significance of the questions in it, sidesteps the question of David's identity and recalls its similar move in 17:12–15, the description of David's family.

The closing scene in 17:57–58 is grisly as Abner brings David to Saul "with the head of the Philistine in his hand." Saul repeats his question, "Whose son are you, youth?" David's response is to the point, "The son of your servant, Jesse the Bethlehemite." No mention of Goliath's head or of the decisive event that has just occurred. David will later rise in the military, but this will be due to his subsequent success and not to the defeat of Goliath: "David went out and was successful wherever Saul sent him; so that Saul set him over the men of war" (18:5).

At the close of 1 Samuel 17, Saul is already exhibiting his jealousy and fear of David that will dominate him from 1 Samuel 18 on. He is attempting to "put David in his place" by ignoring his feat of arms and his own person, the latter by referring to him as someone's son and as "a youth." Such ignoring of a feat is in character with Saul; he ignores Jonathan's destruction of the Philistine garrison in 1 Samuel 14. I will discuss the full chapter later. Saul's subsequent problems with David as successful army commander are foreshadowed in his sharp exchange with Abner his (unsuccessful?) army commander. On the other hand, Saul's jealousy and fear are not yet aroused. For whatever reason, Saul is sincerely concerned with whose son David is. His single-handed slaughter of Goliath has impressed and amazed Saul, and he is shocked by Abner's ignorance. I will not continue this line of reading with the focus on Saul because it would require a reading of the extensive material on Saul that precedes 1 Samuel 16–17; this is beyond my present scope.

1 Samuel 16–17 end, as they began, by offering reliable and essential knowledge, but by already having withdrawn the offer. The explicit and literal detail in narration, dialogue, and description is not matched by clarity of meaning and significance. At crucial points the text only provides information, or clarification of information, that is already given.

1 Samuel 17: Commentaries

Most of the difficulties and problems that I have been analyzing have been noted in biblical commentaries, but the response to them has been quite different from my reading. As I stated in the

Introduction, my mode of reading is a departure from the main
ways of reading the Bible, particularly their desire for clear and
definite meaning, for meaning that is not marred by inconsistency
and contradiction. When the latter are encountered in the biblical
text, they are somehow removed, reduced to something else, and
overcome in some fashion; all the modes of reading biblical
narrative that I am familiar with share the characteristic of ignoring
or denying the specific text.

A conservative commentary, such as that of Keil and Delitzsch,
maintains the historical and literal inerrancy of the biblical text.
They therefore argue strenuously against any assumption that the
problems in the text stem from a later compilation or edition of
earlier sources, traditions, or such, that derive from different times,
places, and authors. For them the text is one and it is inerrant. But
Keil and Delitzsch do respond to the problems that lead to source
and redactional hypotheses with analogous attempts to produce a
definitive, univocal reading, and their modes of interpretation are
instructive.

At times, Keil and Delitzsch simply ignore the problem; they do
not comment on it. In a lengthy footnote, they discuss some of the
source hypotheses offered for 1 Samuel 17 and the evidence presented to support the hypotheses. The footnote concludes with an
analysis of the meeting between Saul, Abner, and David—an analysis to which I will return—and closes with the comment: "The other
difficulties [of 1 Samuel 17] are trivial, and will be answered in connection with the exposition of the passages in question" (Samuel,
178). Following is their exposition of the "two endings" of the
David and Goliath duel in 17:50-51:

> Ver. 50 contains a remark by the historian with reference
> to the result of the conflict: *"Thus David was stronger than
> the Philistine with sling and stone, and smote the Philis-
> tine, and slew him without a sword in his hand."* And then
> in ver. 51 the details are given, namely, that David cut off
> the head of the fallen giant with his own sword. (184; their
> italics)

Vs. 51 is not cited literally as is vs. 50, and the contradiction is not
mentioned, only the cutting off of Goliath's head. The problem has
been effectively "removed" by being ignored.

Another interpretative technique is evident when Keil and
Delitzsch note the length and detail of the narrative in 1 Samuel 17
and state that in the style "the intention is very apparent to set forth

most distinctly the marvellous overruling of all the circumstances by God himself" (176). The foregoing close reading of 1 Samuel 17 revealed that God's "marvellous overruling" was introduced as a theme in David's speeches to the men of Israel, to Saul, and to Goliath, but was then not confirmed by God himself nor by the narration. Indeed, the appeal to the Lord may have been made by David only for its public effect. Finally, it is only one theme of the chapter among many others. Keil and Delitzsch have thus proceeded to take just one theme of the story, a theme whose function and significance are uncertain, and have made it into "the intention" of the text, an intention that is "set forth most distinctly." This is an example of what I have termed interpretation by univocal assertion in which other possibilities, equivocations, ambiguities, etc., are disposed of by positing just one aspect of the narrative as "the meaning" and as a meaning that is not contaminated by inconsistency and contradiction.

In line with this mode of reading, Keil and Delitzsch offer little evidence or argument to support their above assertion. Their sole comment employs a reasoning already noted in Vawter's commentary on Gen 12:10–20 (41–42); the following citation continues directly the above citation.

> And this circumstantiality of the account is closely connected with the form of the narrative, which abounds in repetitions, that appear to us tautological in many instances, but which belong to the characteristic peculiarities of the early Hebrew style of historical composition. (176)

Thus "early Hebrew style" signifies "early Hebrew style": it is not to be questioned further for implications, significance, etc.

Another approach to overcoming the text is to rewrite the narrative so that the new narrative, the rewritten story, will not contain the problems, gaps, etc., of the original or will have enough added material to account for them in a new setting. Keil and Delitzsch analyze the end of the David and Goliath story by making a lengthy "addition" to it. They recognize that the closing conversation is troublesome because "Saul himself could not well have forgotten that David was a son of the Bethlehemite Jesse" (178). They proceed to rewrite the scene. Saul does not want to know just the name of David's father, but also wants to find out "what kind of man the father of a youth who possessed the courage to accomplish so marvellous a heroic deed was" (178). Saul "in all probability" would want such a man attached to his court. The commentators recognize that the "rewriting" is stretching the textual evidence:

> It is true that David merely replied, "the son of thy servant Jesse of Bethlehem;" but it is very evident from the expression in ch. xviii.1, "when he had made an end of speaking unto Saul," that Saul conversed with him still further about his family affairs, since the very words imply a lengthened conversation. (178)

If Keil and Delitzsch cannot ignore it as with 17:50–51, then they supplement it and rewrite it. And they assert their point, they do not argue it: "it is very evident from the expression . . . that . . ." and "the very words imply. . . ."

Peter Ackroyd's Cambridge Bible Commentary, *The First Book of Samuel* (1971), and P. Kyle McCarter's more recent Anchor Bible commentary, *I Samuel* (1980), are both lengthy and up-to-date expositions of standard source and redactional hypotheses of the composition of 1 Samuel. Neither Ackroyd nor McCarter is troubled, as are Keil and Delitzsch, by the assumption that the biblical text derives from different authors or traditions which could have diverse, and sometimes contradictory, views on the same events and characters and which could have been motivated by radically different reasons for telling the same story. They do not feel compelled to defend the historical or literal inerrancy of 1 Samuel.

However, like Keil and Delitzsch, Ackroyd and McCarter are troubled by the presence of inconsistencies, contradictions, etc., within the work of one "author" or tradition and therefore must regard the presence of such difficulties as evidence that the "work" under consideration, e.g., 1 Samuel 17, is not the product of one "author," but of two or more. All three commentaries share the need to produce clear, univocal readings, to demonstrate the intention, the purpose, of the narrative in 1 Samuel. They differ, although not radically, in the ways in which they proceed to produce their own definitive interpretations. The issue is not who will deal with the specific text, but how it will be overcome by each commentator.

Neither Ackroyd nor McCarter print 1 Samuel 17 as a single, unbroken text in their respective commentaries, but both divide it into different sections or stories which they then can comment on separately. In the first part I noted this effect as one shared by most biblical commentaries (23). In McCarter's book such "stories" or sections are further dissected by printing some verses in italics to mark them as later editorial additions. Such source and redactional analysis recognizes difficulties, peculiarities, inconsistencies, and such, but negates their effect on reading by relegating them to secondary status, by considering them as evidence for the disintegration of the text, not as material to be incorporated into a reading of the text.

A thorough reading of the biblical text is blocked by the division of the text into other separate and independent texts. However, the latter "texts" in turn are not subjected to a thorough reading, but are dealt with in ways that are analogous to those employed by Keil and Delitzsch. Again, the issue is not whether the specific text with its details, lacunae, etc., will be read or not; the issue is how and at what point in the analysis the specific text will be put aside and replaced by or reduced to other "texts." In historical-critical commentaries such as those of Ackroyd and McCarter, the biblical text is frequently replaced by "history," both of the formation and composition of the biblical text ("tradition-history") and also of Israel, here in 1 Samuel the rise of the early monarchy.

Such "history" usually results in the rewriting of the biblical text. This is accomplished either by taking material away because it "does not fit with" the specific verses being analyzed or by adding material in the form of historical conjectures. The conjectures concern "what really happened" but was not reported in 1 Samuel, or how such supposedly disparate material ever got combined to form 1 Samuel. This is analogous to Keil and Delitzsch's "rewriting" of the end of 1 Samuel 17. It would be interesting and rewarding to analyze Ackroyd's and McCarter's commentaries in terms of the amount of space devoted to such "historical" enterprises in comparison with the space given to reading the texts themselves.

One of the main independent and unified accounts identified in the Books of Samuel is the History of David's Rise, HDR in abbreviation. McCarter states that it extends from 1 Sam 16:14 through 2 Sam 5:10 (27–30). Nevertheless, the account itself is not regarded as a separate document from one author; there are too many repetitions, inconsistencies, and contradictions for that. The theory, of McCarter and others, is that there was an original document which now "underlies" 1 Samuel 16–2 Samuel 5; it was probably written at the time of David himself and related his rise to the kingship of both Judah and Israel. The document then went through various

redactional "up-datings" by means of the addition of other material
and parallel stories that varied greatly in length. The "up-datings"
reveal themselves because they repeat other material and are incon-
sistent with it or because in some manner they contrast with their
immediate context.

  HDR was not written, according to McCarter, just because of
"the antiquarian impulse of its author." There was another purpose,
"to show the legitimacy of David's succession to Saul as rightful
king of all Israel, north as well as south." The demonstration of
David's legitimacy was "worked out against a theological background in which David is envisioned as Yahweh's chosen king and
Saul as the king abandoned by Yahweh" (28). The assertion is com-
parable to Keil and Delitzsch's "marvellous overruling of all the
circumstances by God himself." McCarter's analysis of HDR has to
presume, has to conjecture, "conservative elements . . . who were
suspicious of the new king." HDR, therefore, offers "rebuttal to
charges made against David" (29). The "purposes" isolated by Mc-
Carter guide his reading of 1 Samuel 16 on, and analogous ones
guide Ackroyd's, although he does not explicitly develop them.

  But my reading of just 1 Samuel 16–17 has already demon-
strated that although the themes mentioned immediately above are
possible themes or "purposes" of the narrative, they cannot be
asserted to be the essential and core meaning or meanings of the
narrative without doing violence to the text. Indeed, some of the
themes, e.g., the concept of "Yahweh's chosen king," were found to
be empty of significance. The above theory of HDR is another
excellent example of asserting that one possible part of a narrative,
and a part with uncertain status and function in the narrative, is the
core, the purpose, of the narrative. The rest of the narrative is then
accommodated to this or ignored in one manner or another. In my
continuing readings, I will comment occasionally on similar modes
of avoiding the text itself.

1 Samuel 17 and Related Texts

  What is to be made of a duel that has two outcomes and in
which the identity of one of the combatants is not certain? Does
David or Elhanan kill Goliath, or are there two Goliaths? What
significance does the battle with Goliath have? It provides no
explicit clarification of the events of 1 Samuel 16, and it has little or
nothing to do with what follows in 1 Samuel 18 on. David is not
rewarded by promotion, money, or marriage to the king's daughter.

The women praise him as he returns from the conflict, but it is not certain, mainly because of the numbers mentioned in their brief song, that the praise is for the defeat of Goliath; in any case, their song results in Saul's jealousy, not in a reward for David (18:6–9).

Jacob's nocturnal wrestling match in Gen 32:23–33 (Engl. 32:22–32) represents an inversion of the David and Goliath duel. The episode has two beginnings as Jacob crosses the Jabbok with his family, or he does not cross the Jabbok himself, but does send his family across:

> (23) The same night he [Jacob] arose and took his two wives, his two maids, and his eleven children, and crossed [3rd masc. sing.] the ford of the Jabbok. (24) He took them and sent them across the stream, and likewise everything that he had [Engl. 22–23].

Roland Barthes has noted the ambiguity in his study of the episode (1974, esp. 23–26). He relates it to two different ways of reading the ensuing conflict. If Jacob has not crossed the river, then the conflict is a test of battle to earn the right to cross the river. If he has crossed the river, then he is marked or branded by his solitude— "And Jacob was left alone" (32:25)—and by the lameness resulting from his conflict: "he touched the hollow of his thigh; and Jacob's thigh was put out of joint as he wrestled with him . . . he passed Penuel, limping because of his thigh" (32:26–32). I note that the different modes of reading the tale are both supported by the text at the same time; it is both . . . and, not either . . . or.

With either ending of the David and Goliath duel, David has passed a test of battle and is marked.

> So David prevailed over the Philistine with a sling and with a stone, and struck the Philistine, and killed him; there was no sword in the hand of David. Then David ran and stood over the Philistine, and took his sword and drew it out of its sheath, and killed him, and cut off his head with it. (1 Sam 17:50–51)

The question is, what are the test and the mark of? Is there a manifestation of the Lord's power, of the fact that David is the Lord's anointed? Is this just the first sign that David is a man of violence, a man of the sword? Or is it a test and mark of something else? Nevertheless, even this equivocation is rendered more problematic by the text in 2 Samuel 21: who actually fought and killed Goliath? Who was tested? Who was marked?

The ambiguity between David and Elhanan finds a counterpart in the difficulty in identifying Jacob's assailant. Is he some super-natural being, God himself, or perhaps even a manifestation of Esau? After the encounter, Jacob says, "I have seen God face to face, and yet my life is preserved" (Gen 32:31). When the assailant changes Jacob's name to Israel, he asserts, "for you have striven with God and with men, and have prevailed" (32:29). In the following chapter, Jacob meets Esau after a twenty year absence and proclaims to Esau, "to see your face is like seeing the face of God" (33:10).

The lack of significance of the David and Goliath episode for the ensuing story of David is matched by a similar undecidability in the association of the incident of Jacob's wrestling with the rest of the Jacob narrative. No other mention is made of the wrestling, of Jacob's resultant lameness, or of the prohibition against eating "the sinew of the hip which is on the hollow of the thigh" (32:33). In Gen 35:10, God changes Jacob's name to Israel with no mention of the same change that was pronounced by the man in Gen 32:28–29. In both 1 Samuel 17 and Gen 32:23–33, there are stories which offer much, but whose significance is undecidable; much can be conjectured, but nothing can be asserted definitively without sup-pressing the text in some manner.

In any case, David stands in association with Jacob because of the parallel duel episodes and because both are, in their own ways, God's "elect." There is then reason to expect other parallels between Jacob and David. Full reading of Jacob's wrestling at the Jabbok would require incorporation of the Lord's attack on Moses in Exod 4:24–26. Both conflicts occur in similar settings as the main charac-ters are returning to their people and are subjected to mysterious attacks at night at a lodging place; the Hebrew *lyn*, "to spend the night," occurs in Gen 32:22 and Exod 4:24. Both episodes stand in an indeterminate relation to their context. The Moses episode is thereby indirectly related to the David and Goliath story; the for-mer has already been connected with the David narrative through its incorporation into the "paradigm" of husband, wife, and third party tales which include 1 Samuel 25 and 2 Samuel 11–12 (see above, 27–28).

In my previous treatment of the "paradigm" of stories (see above, 27–30; 33–35; 38–40), I focused on the prevalence of the theme of violence in most of the tales. Although the theme is important to the stories, individually and as a series, they cannot be reduced to it without ignoring and suppressing the specific details of each story, without doing violence to the text. Vice versa, for a theme to be generally applicable, it must be abstract, and the more abstract the theme, the concept, the emptier of content. With this caution in mind, I will again focus on the theme of violence, on its occurrence in the events of 1 Samuel 17, and on the allusions to it in the specific terminology and phraseology employed in the narration. Violence has already been associated with David in my reading of the young man's description of him in 1 Sam 16:18; the association occurs through a network of analogies and allusions (see above, 55–57).

When Saul finally consents to let David fight Goliath, he arms him with his own armor, including a sword. David is not used to the armor, "and David put them off" (17:39). The first explicit connection of David with the sword, the symbol of violence, concludes with separation. The Hebrew root employed for "to put off" is *swr*, and it is used elsewhere to denote separation, sometimes definitive separation. In 16:14, the Spirit of the Lord departs from Saul; in 16:23 the Evil Spirit departs from Saul after David's lyre playing. In the latter instance, however, the Spirit will return. In 18:12 and 28:15–16, mention is again made of God's departure from Saul. 18:12 is followed immediately by the note that "Saul removed [*swr*] him [David] from his presence" (18:13). God's departure in 18:12 is final; David's is not. 28:15 reports Saul's own admission that God has turned from him; the admission is immediately confirmed by Samuel's shade, "the Lord has turned from you and become your enemy" (28:16).

In his first reported speech, David speaks of "the man who kills this Philistine, and takes away [*swr*] the reproach from Israel" (17:26). Subsequently he threatens Goliath, "I will strike you down, and cut off [*swr*] your head" (17:46). Beheading, a violent and definitive act, is comparatively frequent in the David story: David beheads Goliath (17:51), the Philistines behead Saul (31:9), Baanah and Rechab behead (*swr*) Ishbosheth (2 Sam 4:7), Abishai threatens to behead (*swr*) Shimei (2 Sam 16:9), and the people of Abel of Beth-maacah behead Sheba (2 Sam 20:22). The only other beheading in Genesis–2 Kings occurs in Gen 40:18–20. Pharaoh's chief baker is beheaded in fulfillment of Joseph's interpretation of his dream. The Joseph story is never far from a reading of the David story.

David "puts off" Saul's armor, including the sword, but the separation is not final since David makes good on his threat to Goliath and cuts off his head with the Philistine's own sword. At a later point in the narrative, David arms himself with this very sword, "the sword of Goliath the Philistine, whom you killed in the valley of Elah" (1 Sam 21:10 [Engl. 21:9]). But before this arming and shortly after the defeat of Goliath, "Jonathan stripped himself of the robe that was upon him, and gave it to David, and his armor, and even his sword (18:4). Apparently David accepts them. Over and above allusions to the transfer of royal power from Saul's house to David (Jobling), there are also allusions to the violence that will accompany David and his family and the violence that will engulf Saul and Jonathan.

Jonathan gives David his robe (18:4; Heb.: *mĕ'îl*). Samuel has a similar robe which was first given him by his mother (2:19) and which goes with him to the grave (28:14).

> As Samuel turned to go away, Saul laid hold upon the skirt of his robe, and it tore. And Samuel said to him, "The Lord has torn the kingdom of Israel from you this day." (15:27–28)

The robe is a symbol of the kingdom of Israel. In 1 Samuel 24, David is presented with an opportunity to kill Saul, but he does not.

> Then David arose and steathily *cut off* the skirt of Saul's robe. And afterward David's heart smote him, because he had *cut off* Saul's skirt . . . And David said to Saul, . . . See, my father, see the skirt of your robe in my hand; for by the fact that I *cut off* the skirt of your robe and did not kill you, you may know and see that there is no wrong or treason in my hands. (24:5–12 [Engl. 4–11])

A future reading will have to assess the impact of "the robe" as a symbol of the kingdom of Israel and will also have to follow the various other threads in the citation, e.g., "cutting off" and "knowing and seeing." Faced with the evidence of the piece of his robe, Saul admits to David that "you are more righteous than I; for you have repaid me good, whereas I have repaid you evil" (24:18 [Engl. 17]). He concedes that David "shall surely be king, and that the kingdom of Israel shall be established *in your hand*" (24:21). ("See, my father, see the skirt of your robe *in my hand*.") Finally, Saul has David swear that he "will not *cut off* my descendants after me" (24:22).

"And Jonathan stripped himself of the robe that was upon him." Saul "too stripped off his clothes, and he too prophesied before Samuel, and lay naked all that day and all that night"

(19:24). (The passage will be read in more detail and in context later.) "On the morrow, when the Philistines came to strip the slain, they found Saul and his three sons fallen on Mount Gilboa. And they cut off his head, and stripped off his armor" (31:8–9). The text needs no further comment. Terms such as "robe," "cut off," "strip," etc., which are apparently straightforward descriptions, implicate the theme of violence by a web of analogies; following them through the biblical narrative would create other intricate mazes.

David girds himself with a sword, but then puts it off (17:39). He dissociates himself from this symbol of violence, at least for a short while. After the adultery with Bathsheba and the murder of her husband Uriah, Nathan the prophet quotes the Lord's pronouncement of punishment, "Thus says the Lord . . . Now therefore the sword shall never depart [*swr*] from your house" (2 Sam 12:7–10). Previous to this, the Lord himself spoke to Nathan and sent him to tell David, "Thus says the Lord of hosts . . . I will raise up your offspring after you . . . and my steadfast love shall never depart [*swr*] from you, as I took it [*swr*] from Saul, whom I put away [*swr*] from before you" (2 Sam 7:8–15). This is just as Saul had earlier attempted to put David away [*swr*] from before himself (1 Sam 18:13).

The root *swr*, to put off or depart, in 1 Samuel 17 has a "two-edged" allusion to promises of the presence of the Lord's steadfast love (Heb.: *ḥésed*) and of the sword (Heb.: *ḥéreb*). Neither can be "put off." Future reading of the parallel texts, especially of the "dynastic oracle" in 2 Sam 7:4–17, will have to account for the entire text and the context. For the "dynastic oracle," this will include the speech of the man of God to Eli in 1 Sam 2:27–36 with particular attention to vs. 30 where the Lord is quoted as canceling an "eternal promise." The reading will also entail the Lord's "change of mind" in 1 Sam 15:10–35. How "eternal" can the dynastic promise be? In the text of the oracle, the Lord refers to giving Israel their own place where they will "be disturbed no more; and violent men shall afflict them no more, as formerly . . . and I will give you rest from all your enemies" (2 Sam 7:10–11). This does not correspond to the continuing narrative in the books of Samuel and Kings since Israel is constantly afflicted by violent men; the lack of correspondence thereby puts into question the status of the entire oracle.

Finally, there are some interesting parallels to the root *swr* in 2 Samuel 22 and 1 Kings 15. In the song he sings "on the day when the Lord delivered him from the hand of all his enemies, and from the hand of Saul" (2 Sam 22:1), David asserts that "all his ordinances were before me, and from his statutes I did not turn aside [*swr*]" (22:23). The assertion contrasts sharply with the depiction of David in 1 and 2 Samuel. Nevertheless, it is later confirmed in the narration: "David did what was right in the eyes of the Lord, and did not turn aside [*swr*] from anything that he commanded him all the days of his life, except in the matter of Uriah the Hittite" (1 Kgs 15:5). Such texts render futile any attempt to reduce the reading to one theme or set of themes. Indeed, the foregoing tracing of selected themes and terms demonstrates the explosion of biblical narrative; one text leads not just to another along a straight path, but to many others and along intricate, winding paths.

Violence cannot serve as the meaning, the center, of the reading. Violence there is in the texts, but it is always in the form of specific acts of violence, and it is predicated of all the major characters and groups of characters: of Goliath and the Philistines, of Saul and his family, of David and his house, and of the Lord himself. To render violence a general theme that encompasses the entire reading is to abstract it from the texts or to reduce the texts to it. However, abstraction and reduction share the characteristic of emptiness. The more abstract, the more general, is a theme, the less its specific content. The narrative text with all its details, gaps, and undecidable features is put aside, is resolved, in favor of an important, but empty, theme. The whole, the narrative, is replaced by one of its parts, a theme.

My reading remains undecided. I will not resolve it by convicting David of sin, of cunning, and effective scheming to attain the throne. This goes beyond the specific evidence that the text provides for the characterization of David. The narrative raises the questions of David's motivations and intentions, both immediate and future, but leaves them indeterminate. David is a cunning and unscrupulous schemer, and he is also an innocent "man of destiny" for whom all goes right. The text supports a spectrum of portrayals of David and thereby does not support any one definitive or probable portrayal.

1 Samuel 18: Betrothal and Blood

To return to the text, 1 Sam 18:1–6 is composed of short, juxtaposed sections. The events transpire on the day of the defeat of

Goliath (18:1–2, 6) or shortly thereafter (18:10). We are also informed of David's longer term success and its results, his promotion to army commander and also the fear and jealousy of Saul (18:5, 12–16). The section is framed by an inclusion since vss. 1 and 16 both speak of someone loving David, first Jonathan and then all Israel and Judah. Jonathan makes a covenant with David "because he loved him as himself" (18:3). Commentaries note that "to love" refers not just to personal affection, but also to political loyalty and commitment (e.g., McCarter, 305)/8/. However, the biblical narrative says nothing more, at this point, of the covenant or of the "love." In 1 Samuel 20, a covenant between David and Jonathan will be spelled out in more detail.

Saul's anger and jealousy are so intense that he attempts to kill David twice (18:10–11). The attempts are unsuccessful, and Saul then resorts to an indirect approach. He offers David his eldest daughter Merab as a wife if David will be valiant, or one of his valiant warriors (McCarter, 301 and 306), and fight the battles of the Lord. That is what Saul says to David, but to himself he says, "Let not my hand be upon him, but let the hand of the Philistines be upon him" (18:17). I commented above on the passage's relation to the purported offer of a royal reward for the slaughter of Goliath (17:25; see 64).

David responds, "Who am I, and who are my kinsfolk, my father's family in Israel, that I should be son-in-law to the king?" (18:18). As is so frequently the case with David's "questions," the status of David's response cannot be decided. Is it a rhetorical question, a statement that he is not worthy to be the king's son-in-law? Or is it a literal question? David is sincerely concerned whether or not he is worthy to be the king's son-in-law. Even if we read it as a rhetorical question, we then face the problem of whether to take the assertion as sincere or insincere. Does David truly feel unworthy, or is he saying this just to bide his time, not to "make his move" prematurely? Leaving David aside, what does Saul hear and respond to? Does he hear a sincere statement of David's unworthiness, a question of his worthiness, or a veiled, uncertain response?

The text does not resolve the problem. "And when it was time to give Merab, Saul's daughter, to David, she was given to Adriel" (18:19; McCarter, 301). David is and is not sincere in his statement; Saul is giving Merab to Adriel with David's knowledge and consent and as an unexpected insult to David. "But at the time when Merab, Saul's daughter, *should have been given to David*, she was given to Adriel the Meholathite for a wife" (18:19; *RSV*). At an important point in the narrative, the narration does not provide information on Saul's thoughts and reactions; I noted a similar reticence in 17:31–40. In any case, David does not fall in battle with the Philistines, and Saul refines his scheme when opportunity next offers itself.

I take this opportunity to digress into a brief discussion of the Hebrew text and the differing translations of it in Bibles and commentaries, particularly those in *RSV* and McCarter. This is not a treatise on translation. Most of the biblical passages that I cite are from the *RSV* with no change. At times, I do change a word or a phrase, not to improve or alter the translation, but to indicate more clearly that the passage in question shares the word or phrase with another passage. For example, in 17:55, in Abner's response to Saul, I replaced "I cannot tell" of the *RSV* with "I do not know" to make explicit the theme of knowledge. On a few occasions I offer a translation different from that in the *RSV* because I do not accept their translation for one reason or another. For example, in 17:12 I make no emendation of the text as in the *RSV* and offer a translation of the Hebrew text as it stands (58). In 17:58 I omit the "I am" of the *RSV* because it is not in the Hebrew text, and its omission accords with David's other statements in 1 Samuel 17 which keep his own person in the background. Finally, I frequently change a "then," a "for," a "because," etc., in the *RSV* to an "and." This brings me to the two translations of 18:19 from McCarter and the *RSV*.

In this instance, it is not necessarily a matter of a better or more accurate translation, but a matter of how to translate a Hebrew text that is ambiguous and equivocal. As I have argued previously, the text can support both the "and" (chance) and the "should have" (necessity), both McCarter's and the *RSV*'s translations of 18:19. The text is therefore undecidable on the question of whether Merab should have been given to David. At times I may replace a "for," a "because," etc., with an "and" in an attempt to translate the undecidability of the Hebrew text. However, this entails the possibility that the translation may then positively reflect an interpretation of the events as related solely by coincidence, i.e., a decided and definitive interpretation in its own right. Frequently I therefore present or discuss alternate translations.

I return to the reading of 1 Samuel 18 with focus on the offer of Michal to David as wife (vss. 20–29). Saul is informed that his youngest daughter Michal has fallen in love with David, and this time he does not leave a military encounter with the Philistines to chance. The proposal to become the king's son-in-law is again conveyed to David. There are three characters or groups involved, Saul, David, and Saul's servants who act as messengers between the first two. Nothing is said about why messengers are needed; apparently David is not at court. David responds to Saul's servants' first speech with a "question," "Does it seem to you a little thing to become the king's son-in-law, seeing that I am a poor man and of no repute?" (18:23). The "question" is repeated to Saul, and he immediately sends his servants back with an appropriate rejoinder to what he apparently has heard as David's doubts about his worthiness and about his ability to pay a bride-price or marriage present; "The king desires no marriage present except a hundred foreskins of the Philistines, that he may be avenged of the king's enemies" (18:25). The narrative comments immediately, "Now Saul thought to make David fall by the hand of the Philistines." Saul's condition, the requested marriage present, is reported back to David, and he "saw it as an opportunity to offer himself as a son-in-law to the king" (18:26; McCarter, 315).

The comment demonstrates that David's initial response to Saul's servants expressed sincere concerns about his worthiness to be the king's son-in-law, especially his ability to provide an appropriate marriage present. Or it demonstrates nothing about the initial response. Whatever he may have meant then, David now sees "an opportunity" offered in Saul's counter-proposal. (An "opportunistic" David was suggested above in the reading of 1 Samuel 17 [68].) David has been negotiating with Saul with no set goal in mind and has been keeping himself and his desires in the background with the hope that something to his advantage would emerge from the discussions. In either case, he goes with his men, kills 200 Philistines, and returns their foreskins to Saul as the marriage present. David is given Michal as his wife, but Saul's plan has failed; he "was still more afraid of David . . . [and] was David's enemy continually" (18:29).

The Lord is still with David, and his success increases.

> Then the princes of the Philistines came out to battle, and as often as they came out David had more success than all the servants of Saul; so that his name was highly esteemed. (18:30)

Alter has noted the parallel with the Joseph story in Genesis 39 which similarly begins and ends with descriptions of the "hero's success, God's being with him, and his popularity" (1978: 59). The parallel is not surprising; I have noted others with the Joseph story in 1 Samuel 17 and in the reference to David's good looks in the description of him in 1 Sam 16:18; indeed, the latter alludes to Genesis 39/9/. The analogies with the Joseph narrative raise expectations that David will be another Joseph and that his story will likewise end in peace and reconciliation, but the expectations are not realized. The analogy with Joseph is complicated and upset by a more specific, although inverted, parallel with the Jacob story.

Like David, Jacob becomes another man's son-in-law. The man is Laban, Jacob's uncle, and he has two daughters; "the name of the older was Leah, and the name of the younger was Rachel" (Gen 29:16). "Jacob loved Rachel"; this contrasts with "Michal loved David." Jacob serves Laban seven years as a "marriage present" for her, but at the time of the wedding, Laban switches daughters and gives the eldest daughter, Leah, to Jacob. Laban cites a local custom in his self-defense "It is not so done in our country, to give the younger before the first-born" (Gen 29:26). This may or may not be the case in Haran, but the explanation does serve to stress the lack of a similar reason to explain Saul's giving Merab, his eldest daughter, to Adriel. Jacob then also marries Rachel and has to serve another seven years, i.e., double the original marriage price, for her (29:15–30). In the ensuing years, Leah bears six sons to Jacob and an additional two through her maid, Zilpah; Rachel bears only two sons and an additional two through her maid Bilhah. Rachel herself dies giving birth to her second son Benjamin ((35:16–19).

When Jacob is fleeing from Laban to return to Canaan (Genesis 31), Rachel steals her father's "teraphim," apparently some type of idols, and then lies about the theft. In 1 Sam 19:11–17, when David is fleeing from Saul, Michal deceives her father's servants by putting "teraphim" in David's bed, thereby making them believe that David is there. Alter has noted the parallel with Genesis and comments, "Perhaps the allusion is meant to foreshadow a fatality shared by Michal with Rachel, who becomes the object of Jacob's unwitting curse because of the theft" (1978: 61). Jacob's "curse" is spoken to Laban, "Anyone with whom you find your gods shall not live" (Gen 31:32). I see no reason to qualify the statement with a "perhaps."

Merab the eldest is given to another, and David marries Michal the youngest. This stands in an inverted relationship with Jacob's marriage to both Leah, the eldest and the most fertile, and Rachel, the youngest. Jacob's marriages produce thirteen children, including Dinah; this is a blessing for himself and for Laban. David's marriage to Michal produces no children; this is a neutral consequence or perhaps a blessing for himself, but certainly a curse for Saul. The dealings between Jacob and Laban and then between Jacob and his wives over children involve cunning and deception, but they do not involve violence. As is to be expected with David, his dealings with Saul and his two daughters entail violence; he slaughters 200 Philistines and cuts off their foreskins.

Killing Philistines in order to obtain a marriage present finds an analogy in Samson who kills thirty Philistines to take their garments to pay off the "riddling bet" made during his wedding feast (Judg 14:10–20). Samson has already been drawn into the network of analogies surrounding David through the previous discussion of David's possession by the the Spirit of the Lord (above: 53). As in the cases of Jacob and David, an elder and a younger daughter are involved. Samson's wife, the elder daughter, is taken from him (Judg 14:20), and he is subsequently offered the younger, but he refuses her (15:1–3). The Samson saga is marked by violence that is usually murderous and illogical. Did Samson really need to kill the Philistines to take their garments? He is frequently possessed by the Spirit of the Lord which apparently urges him on to some of his murderous acts (e.g., Judg 14:19). Yet Samson's violence has no extensive or lasting effects. Indeed, he kills more Philistines at his death than during his life (16:30). He apparently dies childless. Is there a lesson here for David and his house which are similarly given to violence? Is David impelled in his violence against the Philistines by the Spirit of the Lord and by "hot anger"? (Judg 14:19). Or is David like Jacob and Laban, cunning and sagacious, always aware of what he is doing and of any opportunities that may be presented?

In another article, "Biblical Type-Scenes and the Uses of Convention," Alter focuses on the specific type-scene of the "encounter with the future betrothed at a well" and discusses some of the texts, or closely related ones, that I have been analyzing. He describes the betrothal type-scene as follows:

> . . . [it] must take place with the future bridegroom, or his
> surrogate, having journeyed to a foreign land. There he
> encounters a girl . . . or girls at a well. Someone, either the

man or the girl, then draws water from the well; afterward,
the girl or girls rush to bring home the news of the
stranger's arrival . . . ; finally, a betrothal is concluded
between the stranger and the girl, in the majority of
instances, only after he has been invited to a meal.
(359)/10/

Alter's analysis focuses on the encounter between Abraham's servant
and Rebekah in Gen 24:10–61, Jacob's meeting Rachel in Gen
29:1–20, Moses' meeting Zipporah in Exod 2:15–21, and the
betrothal of Ruth and Boaz in the book of Ruth. In briefer fashion,
he mentions an allusion to the type-scene in 1 Sam 9:11–12 when
Saul and his servant, on their way to see Samuel, "met young maid-
ens coming out to draw water"; and they tell Saul to "make haste!"
Finally, Alter notes the absence of the type-scene in the narrative of
Samson's betrothal and marriage in Judges 14.

He makes the following comment on the betrothals of David in
1 and 2 Samuel:

> We might note that the three discriminated premarital epi-
> sodes in the David cycle all involve bloodshed, in an
> ascending order of moral questionability: the 200 Philistines
> he slaughters in battle as the bride-price for Michal; his
> threat to kill Nabal, Abigail's husband, who then con-
> veniently dies of shock; and his murder of the innocent
> Uriah after having committed adultery with Bathsheba. Are
> these betrothals by violence a deliberate counterpoint to the
> pastoral motif of betrothal after the drawing of water?
> Perhaps, though from this distance in time it is hard to be
> sure. (367)

In passing I would note that David "killed two hundred of the Philistines" (1 Sam 18:27); nothing is said of "in battle." Also, Nabal
does not "conveniently die of shock"; he is struck by the Lord and
dies (1 Sam 25:38).

There is a brief episode in 2 Sam 23:13–17 that contains some
of the elements of Alter's betrothal type-scene and that relates in
other direct and indirect ways to the text under consideration,
1 Sam 18:17–29, the marriage to Michal. Tracing the threads of the
relationships will construct a rather complicated web or webs of
analogies. The episode in question is one of the group of narratives
and poems gathered together in 2 Samuel 21–24, and its relation to
the chronological sequence of the David story is not certain.

> And three of the thirty chief men went down, and came
> about harvest time to David at the cave of Adullam, when a
> band of Philistines was encamped in the valley of Rephaim.
> David was then in the stronghold; and the garrison of the
> Philistines was then at Bethlehem. (2 Sam 23:13–14)

Evidently the Philistines are encamped at Rephaim which is near
Jerusalem, and David is at his stronghold by the cave of Adullam in
southern Judah (1 Sam 22:1), unless another stronghold is meant.
There is also a garrison of Philistines at Bethlehem, over and above
those encamped at Rephaim. The geographical location is reminiscent of the battles between David and the Philistines which are
narrated in 2 Sam 5:15–25. These occurred shortly after David had
been anointed king of Israel (2 Sam 5:17). Perhaps this is the occasion when the events related in 2 Sam 23:13–17 transpired. Or they
may have happened much earlier when David was fleeing from
Saul and was at the cave of Adullam (1 Sam 22:1–2). Or, finally, it
may be an episode similar to that in 2 Samuel 5, but which happened much later in David's life, after the events of 2 Samuel 5–20.

While in the stronghold, David "desires" and says, "O that some
one would give me water to drink from the well of Bethlehem
which is by the gate" (2 Sam 23:15). Three of David's mighty warriors respond immediately, and they "broke through the camp of
the Philistines, and drew water out of the well of Bethlehem which
was by the gate, and took and brought it to David" (23:16). Some of
the elements of Alter's betrothal type-scene are present: "drawing
water from a well" and "giving water to drink." There is a marked
inversion since the well is at Bethlehem, David's home town, and
not at a foreign city.

However, the episode does not continue as a betrothal type-
scene:

> But he [David] would not drink of it; he poured it out to the
> Lord, and said, "Far be it from me, O Lord, that I should
> do this. Shall I drink the blood of the men who went at the
> risk of their lives?" Therefore he would not drink it. (23:17)

The event is usually interpreted as an indication of David's men's
fierce loyalty to him, and of David's appreciation of such loyalty
and daring. Such an interpretation, however, has to exclude the
possibility that the men's daring is in response to a petty desire; it is
not daring, but foolhardiness.

David equates the water that his mighty men have brought to

him with their blood and asks, "Shall I drink the blood of the men who went at the risk of their lives?" No, and he pours the water out "to the Lord." "The value thus put upon it shows David's appreciation of his knights quite as well as if he had drunk their present" (Smith, 385). Or, no, and he pours out their blood onto the ground. "We must all die, we are like water spilt on the ground, which cannot be gathered up again," says the wise woman of Tekoa to Joab (2 Sam 14:14). "The pastoral motif of betrothal after the drawing of water," with the latter reading, changes into a brutal motif of the wanton spilling of blood.

Alter responds to the latter mode of interpretation with "perhaps, though from this distance in time it is hard to be sure" (1978: 367). The theme, Alter's "deliberate counterpoint," is there; that much is "sure." What is not "sure" is that this is the only reading of the texts in question, that David must be convicted of sinfully using violence to attain his own ends, of mindlessly and needlessly spilling others' blood for his own purposes. The "theme" is there; "David" is there. What is not given is the relationship, the association, of the theme and the character.

When David flees from Jerusalem before the attack of Absalom, Shimei, the son of Gera, curses him, "Begone, begone, you man of blood, you worthless fellow! . . . See, your ruin is on you; for you are a man of blood" (2 Sam 16:7–8). At the time, David does not allow Abishai to kill Shimei since the latter's cursing is being done at the Lord's bidding (16:11). But, on his deathbed, David remembers the event somewhat differently; he charges Solomon to "bring his gray head down with blood to Sheol," because he, Shimei, had cursed David with a "grievous curse"; no mention here of any cursing at the Lord's bidding (1 Kgs 2:9). In this context, Shimei's genealogy, he is "a man of the family of the house of Saul" (2 Sam 16:5), may have more bearing on David's order to Solomon. David's charge to Solomon, ending with the mention of blood, is David's last reported words; the very next verse reports his death and burial (1 Kgs 2:10).

The parallel passages are associated with David's slaughter of 200 Philistines. This is his first explicit act of massive blood shed, and it is directly connected to a betrothal, for the 200 foreskins will serve as his marriage present for Michal. Nothing is said in 1 Samuel 18 of the fate of the men who went with David; "David arose and went, along with his men, and killed two hundred of the Philistines" (18:27). Did he pour out their blood on that occasion? Unlike the lone terrorist Samson, most of David's fighting and killing involve others who risk and often lose their own lives.

The above passages furthermore associate foreskins and blood in a system of parallels which involve betrothal. David is to become the king's son-in-law; the Hebrew root employed for becoming a son-in-law is *ḥtn*. The association of foreskins, blood, and *ḥtn* has a parallel in the previously mentioned episode of the Lord's attempt to murder Moses, an attempt that is foiled by his wife Zipporah who "cut off her son's foreskin, and touched his feet with it, and said, 'Surely you are a bridegroom (Heb.: *ḥătan*) of blood to me.' So he let him alone" (Exod 4:25–26). (I note, but do not trace, the thread of "cutting off.") Previously I have included the tale in the "paradigm" of stories of a husband, his wife, and a third party and have also related it to Jacob's nocturnal wrestling match (Gen 32:23–33) which, in turn, is analogous to the David and Goliath story; I am now beginning to come full circle (78–79; 28).

Whatever the brief narrative may mean in its context in the book of Exodus, it is an excellent and enlightening parallel for 1 Samuel 18. Shimei later calls David a "man of blood," in the context of 1 Samuel 18 he is assuredly a "bridegroom of blood" or, more woodenly, a "son-in-law of blood." Again, I emphasize that this is a statement of fact associating a character and a theme or phrase, not necessarily a judgment of character. Both the character and the "title" are given, but their relationship is left open. Future reading will have to assess further other aspects of the parallels between 1 Samuel 18 and the brief tale in Exod 4:24–26.

David marries into Saul's family. The Hebrew verb form employed for "marry into," *hithattēn*, has the same root, *ḥtn*, as "son-in-law." To marry into the royal family David cuts off the foreskins of, i.e., circumcises, 200 dead Philistines. Summarizing the episode in this manner leads to another parallel narrative in the Jacob story, the rape of Dinah narrated in Genesis 34. Here there is also large scale death, although this time the treachery is explicit; "the sons of Jacob answered Shechem and his father Hamor deceitfully, because he had defiled their sister Dinah" (34:13). After the rape, Hamor proclaims to Jacob and his sons that Shechem wishes to marry Dinah, and he appends a surprising proposal. "Make marriages (*hithattēn*) with us; give your daughters to us, and take our daughters for yourselves" (34:9). The sons of Jacob agree, but on one condition:

> We cannot do this thing, to give our sister to one who is
> uncircumcised, for that would be a disgrace to us. Only on

this condition will we consent to you: that you will become
as we are and every male of you be circumcised . . . But if
you will not listen to us and be circumcised, then we will
take our daughter, and we will be gone. (34:14–17)

Immediately preceding this, Shechem had declared, "Ask of me
ever so much as marriage present [Heb.: *mōhar*; see 1 Sam 18:25]
and gift, and I will give according as you say to me" (34:12). Circumcision is associated with the "marriage present" in both Genesis
34 and 1 Samuel 18. In Genesis 34, however, the circumcision is a
ploy and an act that precedes the massacre. "On the third day,
when they were sore, two of the sons of Jacob . . . took their swords
and came upon the city unawares, and killed all the males" (34:25).

A threat of disaster hangs over Jacob and his family since the
slaughter of the Shechemites has brought them trouble and made
them odious to the inhabitants of the land (34:30). Only the intervention of a "terror of God" prevents catastrophe (35:5). David's
slaughter of 200 Philistines has no explicit consequences for David
or for Israel. Indeed, when David flees to Achish of Gath in 1 Sam
21:11–16 (Engl: 10–15), the Philistines recall the couplet sung by
the women to David and Saul in 1 Sam 18:7 on the day of the
defeat of Goliath, a Philistine from Gath, but they do not mention
Goliath or the killing of 200 of their own.

There is an even closer parallel within the David narrative to
the rape of Dinah in the rape of Tamar in 2 Samuel 13. David's
daughter Tamar is raped by her half-brother and David's son
Amnon. Amnon, in turn, is murdered two years later by Absalom,
Tamar's full brother. David, like Jacob, does nothing about the rape
of a daughter. "When David heard of all these things, he was very
angry," but he does and says nothing to Amnon (13:21). The only
action is taken by Absalom. "Now Jacob heard that he [Shechem]
had defiled his daughter Dinah; but his sons were with his cattle in
the field, so Jacob held his peace until they came" (Gen 34:5).
Again, the only action is taken by the sons. The only explicit action
that Jacob takes is to entertain a marriage proposal between Dinah
and Shechem and, indeed, between his entire family and all the
Shechemites. In both stories, rape is described as "a wanton folly"
and "a thing that is not done in Israel" (Gen 34:7 and 2 Sam 13:12).

Genesis 34 is a tale of a brutal massacre that is an overreaction
and also a misplaced reaction. Absalom murders Amnon by deception, but he kills only the one rapist, not the other royal sons,
despite the fears of David; "tidings came to David, 'Absalom has

slain all the king's sons, and not one of them is left'" (2 Sam 13:30). Dinah's brothers, in particular Simeon and Levi, massacre all the men of Shechem through treachery and take the others captive; the entire city dies or is captured because of the one rapist (Gen 34:25–29). The brothers make no overt reaction to the Shechemite's offer of full intermarriage, a proposal that would threaten the very existence of Jacob's whole family, not just the one member. Any threat of intermarriage is averted by the slaughter of the men of the city. Perhaps the brothers view the offer as an opportunity to demand circumcision, and its subsequent period of weakness, of all the men and not just the one, Shechem the rapist. Further, the slaughter results in another threat, i.e., extinction by the other inhabitants of the land. Jacob rebukes his sons for their violence and the consequent situation that they are in.

> Then Jacob said to Simeon and Levi, "You have brought trouble on me by making me odious to the inhabitants of the land, the Canaanites and the Perizzites; my numbers are few, and if they gather themselves against me and attack me, I shall be destroyed, both I and my household." But they said, "Should he treat our sister as a harlot?" (34:30–31)

Their response to their father's rebuke is beside the point since it ignores the brutality and the extent of their reaction to the rape and it ignores the situation that the massacre has left them in.

As with so many of the "questions" that we have encountered in the biblical text, the status of this one is problematic. As a rhetorical question, it asserts that our sister will not be treated as a harlot regardless of the violence of our reaction and of any consequences of that reaction. As a literal question, it could be answered that, under the present circumstances, yes, we will have to let her be treated as a harlot! Or, no, and we will have to find some solution other than a violent reaction.

The threatening consequences that were absent after David's slaughter of 200 Philistines are present after the rape of Tamar and the death of Amnon, but now no "terror of God" will intervene to avert them. In his rebuke to his sons, Jacob speaks of his fear that "I shall be destroyed [Heb.: šāmad], both I and my house" (Gen 34:30). The first news that comes to David of Absalom's murder of Amnon is "Absalom has slain all the king's sons, and not one of them is left" (2 Sam 13:30), except Absalom of course. However, it soon turns out that the opposite has occurred, i.e., only one, Amnon, has died. The deaths of more of David's sons are soon to follow.

When Joab sends the wise woman of Tekoa to David to trick him into allowing Absalom to return from his exile in Geshur, the wise woman speaks first of fratricide since one of her sons has killed her other son. Because of the murder, her family is demanding that the surviving brother, the murderer, should also be put to death, i.e., "they would destroy [Heb.: *šāmad*] the heir also" (2 Sam 14:7). This would leave to her dead husband "neither name nor remnant upon the earth." I note in passing the wide ranging significance in the OT of "name" and "remnant." The wise woman pleads with David that "my son be not destroyed [Heb.: *šāmad*]" (14:11).

2 Samuel 13–14 thereby intone the theme of family violence, including fratricide, that results in only one son or brother surviving. I noted above the occurrence of this state of affairs in the Davidic house with Solomon and Joash (1 Kings 2–11; 2 Kings 11; above, 34–35). The themes of family violence and the sole survivor are already alluded to in David's marriage to Michal, an allusion that works through a network of analogies. Tracing the themes would implicate 1 Samuel 24 again (above, 81); Saul says to David, "Swear to me therefore by the Lord that you will not cut off my descendants after me, and that you will not destroy [*šāmad*] my name out of my father's house" (24:21).

Finally, I point out here the introduction, through the network of analogies, of another "trio": a father who is king, his son, and his army commander. The "trio" has parallels and inversions within its members similar to those in the "paradigm" of a husband, his wife, and a third party. In 1 Samuel, the "trio" is comprised of Saul, Jonathan, and David. Saul wants Jonathan, his son, to kill David, his army commander, but Jonathan does not fulfill his father's wishes (e.g., 1 Sam 19:1–7). In 1 Kings 2, King David commands Solomon, his son, to kill Joab, his army commander, and Solomon efficiently executes the command (1 Kgs 2:5–6, 28–35). In 2 Samuel, the "trio" is composed of David, Absalom, and Joab. David does not want Joab, his army commander, to kill Absalom, his son, but Joab does kill Absalom against David's specific orders (2 Sam 18:1–15). I will incorporate some of the parallel material from 2 Samuel into my reading of 1 Samuel 20, the clandestine meeting between David and Jonathan.

1 Samuel 19: Flight and Escape

No violence befalls David because of his marriage to Michal, so

"Saul spoke to Jonathan his son and to all his servants about killing David" (1 Sam 19:1). Saul returns to the direct approach. But his plan does not succeed because of Jonathan's intercession on David's behalf. Jonathan, having been told by his father of his desire, speaks first to David and is certain, "Saul my father seeks to kill you" (19:2). The following reconciliation between Saul and David (19:7) may obscure this intention for Jonathan, since he apparently has to relearn it in 1 Samuel 20 when Saul attempts to kill him (20:32–34); the present text will be taken into account in my reading of the latter episode. Jonathan tells David to be careful and to "stay in a secret place" (19:2); there is a foreshadowing here of David's sin with Bathsheba which is committed "in a secret place" (2 Sam 12:12).

While David is in the secret place, Jonathan will join his father "in the field" (19:3). This means "outside the city," and may have further significance; "the field" is also the site for the next meeting between Jonathan and David in 1 Samuel 20. Another reading of the David story will have to pay closer attention to the role of setting, both when the setting is specified and when it is not. Jonathan, while with his father in the field, will talk to him about David and then tell David what his father's reaction was (19:3).

Once the plan is set, Jonathan goes to Saul.

> And Jonathan spoke well of David to Saul his father, and
> said to him, "Let not the king sin against his servant David;
> because he has not sinned against you, and because his
> deeds have been of good service to you; for he took his life
> in his hand and he slew the Philistine, and the Lord
> wrought a great victory for all Israel. You saw it, and
> rejoiced; why then will you sin against innocent blood by
> killing David without cause?" (19:4–5)

Jonathan introduces the religious terminology of sin; he uses the term itself three times and speaks also of "innocent blood" and "killing without cause." Such issues have not been raised since the rejection of Saul in 1 Samuel 15, but will be raised again soon in the next encounter between David and Jonathan in 1 Samuel 20. Nevertheless, the issue of sin, however it is to be understood, is not developed here or in 1 Samuel 20, nor is its relation to the context specified. Another reading will have to trace the "thread of sin" through the David story; I note its occurrence in 1 Samuel 24 (see vss. 11–15).

In the middle of his statement to his father, Jonathan refers to

Saul seeing and rejoicing over David's defeat of Goliath and then closes with the appeal, "Why then will you sin against innocent blood by killing David without cause?" Jonathan's statement offers clarity and some added information about the battle with Goliath and Saul's reaction to it, but the text has already withdrawn the offer. "Saul listened to Jonathan's voice [or, speech], and Saul swore, 'As the Lord lives, he shall not be put to death'" (19:6). At this critical juncture, the narration again withholds any comment on Saul's feelings or thoughts, and Saul's oath contains no explanation for itself. Is he convinced by Jonathan's argument or by some part of it? If so, which part? Is it the talk of "sin," the victory over Goliath, or some subtle reminder of the possible consequences of such a violent deed as killing David, his successful and respected army commander? Did Saul, in fact, see and rejoice over David's victory? Or are Jonathan's speech and Saul's oath connected only coincidentally?

Two analogous passages which entail talk of putting someone to death, but with a subsequent reprieve, emphasize the opacity of the present text since they contain some of the information "missing" here. In the aftermath of Saul's victory over the Ammonites, the army demands that they put to death the men who questioned Saul's kingship. Saul rejects the demand, "Not a man shall be put to death this day, *for today the Lord has wrought victory in Israel*" (1 Sam 11:13). Later, the army pleads with Saul to give up a vow that Jonathan, his son, should die because he ate honey in violation of Saul's earlier oath against eating anything on the day of the battle (1 Sam 14:24–30). They speak of Jonathan as he *"who has wrought this great victory* in Israel," and in turn take an oath, "As the Lord lives, there shall not one hair of his head fall to the ground; *for he has wrought with God* this day." The narrative concludes stating why Jonathan did not die: "And the people ransomed Jonathan" (14:45).

David similarly gives up a vow to kill Nabal and his men when Abigail presents him with an argument involving the issue of spilling blood without cause; "my lord shall have no cause of grief, or pangs of conscience, for having shed blood without cause or for my lord taking vengeance himself" (1 Sam 25:31). David may be moved by religious or moral persuasion or by political conviction, i.e., a brutal massacre of Nabal and his men may well come back to haunt him in the future. At other times in the narrative, David shows no compunction to annihilate large groups of people for his own personal gain. For example, while residing with Achish of

Gath, David wipes out entire villages, man, woman, and child, so that none can report back to Achish (1 Sam 27:8–12). Is Saul, in 1 Samuel 19, operating with some such political motives? Does he fear the possible repercussions of killing or alienating such a success-ful general? Or is the reconciliation just a means to get David back to court where Saul can soon make another attempt "to pin David to the wall with the spear"? (19:10).

McCarter's discussion of some of the phrases employed in the scene in 19:1–7 adds some possibilities to the above interpretations. In his Notes on the passage (322), he points out that the phrases, "Jonathan spoke well of David" and "his deeds have been of good service to you," "may carry legal and political nuances in addition to their common meanings." He refers to other studies and to extra-biblical texts to support the contention, and he points to "the reper-toire of covenantal terminology so frequently drawn upon in the stories of Saul, David, and Jonathan." I previously noted the similar added significance of "to love"; "'to love' refers not just to personal affection, but also to political loyalty and commitment" (85–86). There I, in agreement with McCarter, spoke of "legal and political nuances *in addition to* . . . common meanings." However, the text allows us to argue for one meaning exclusive of the other(s), i.e., the text is not supporting a harmonizing view—the third of the follow-ing readings of 18:1–3—as a way of deciding the issue. The first two readings of 18:1–3 are also possible. In 18:1–3, Jonathan loves David only as a personal friend, not as a political ally; he loves him only as a political ally, not as a personal friend; he loves him as both personal friend and political ally. The same range of possibilities holds for Jonathan's "speaking well of David to Saul." Jonathan is speaking in a diplomatic, and not a moral or personal, sense; he is just pointing out to Saul that David "has acted consistently with the loyalty that he owes his king" (McCarter, 322), not that David is a good and righteous man. Like Abigail, Jonathan is employing a very practical, political argument and not a religious or personal appeal. The other possible expositions are evident.

Saul's following attempt to kill David with his spear is the third time that he has tried to "pin David to the wall," and this time David realizes the seriousness of the attempts and flees and escapes (19:9–10). Up to this point in the narrative, we must assume that David has stayed at least in the vicinity of the court, if not actually at court. The dealings with Saul's servants over the proffered hand of Michal indicate that David was not present at the court itself.

Much of the remainder of 1 Samuel is occupied with the various stages of David's "flight and escape" and Saul's corresponding pursuit. It finally ends with David's "escape" to Achish of Gath in 1 Sam 27:1–3. "When it was told Saul that David had fled to Gath, he sought for him no more" (27:4). Michal, Saul's daughter, helps in David's initial flight; the passage was referred to above (87) in association with Alter's treatment of it, particularly the parallels with the story of Rachel.

"Now David fled and escaped, and he came to Samuel at Ramah, and told him all that Saul had done to him" (19:18). But Samuel says nothing in response; indeed, Samuel never speaks to David, here or elsewhere. We are never given a hint of what Samuel thinks of David. The incident at Naioth in Ramah in 19:18–24 is another example of a story told literally and in detail, but a story whose significance in itself and for its context is clouded. One, neither here nor in the parallels in 1 Sam 10:5–13 and 18:10, is the verb "to prophesy" defined. It is not evident what type of behavior is to be understood or imagined by the verb. The second obscurity is the saying quoted at the end of vs. 24.

First, in the parallel in 10:5–13, at least the significance of the action of prophesying is stated. It is a positive sign that Saul "is turned into another man" and given "another heart." The prophesying is a manifestation of the newness. This does not seem to be the case at the end of 1 Samuel 19 where the opposite may be in evidence, a negative sign that Saul is no longer "another man," that he has lost his other heart, that he has lost his kingship (McCarter, 330–31). Such an interpretation fits with the prophesying or "raving" that Saul does after "an evil Spirit of God" has come upon him (18:10). Yet the narration in 19:23–24 says nothing about whether the sign is positive or negative or whether the incident has produced any change in Saul. Above I noted the allusiveness of the phrase "he too stripped off his clothes" (81–82).

The text narrates without comment on either the action or the characters. Nor is any reaction, physical, verbal, or emotional, of Samuel or David reported; Jonathan, who is soon to appear, is not even mentioned. There is no hint as to whether or not Saul's prophesying has changed the state of affairs in effect after David's flight from his house. There is only the impersonal and enigmatic "question" which closes the episode: "Is Saul also among the prophets?" Is this a literal question? Or is it a rhetorical question, an assertion or expression of surprise that Saul is among the prophets? In either case, is it to be understood as praise, condemnation, or a neutral observation? David's first encounter with another person in his flight from Saul is marked by clear narration, but not by clear signification.

1 Samuel 20: Jonathan

David's second encounter is with Jonathan, and it is narrated in quite different fashion from the preceding episode. David's visit with Samuel occupied seven verses; the meeting with Jonathan takes 42 verses. David told Samuel "all that Saul had done to him." David's actual words are not reported, and there is no mention of Samuel's response or even of whether he responded at all. 1 Samuel 20 is dominated by extensive dialogue between David and Jonathan, and Saul and Jonathan; narration is at a minimum. The length of the chapter, coupled with the extensive dialogue, draws attention to the chapter itself. However, the reading will encounter some familiar problems. What is being said and why? What is happening and why? The text supports a range of answers to the questions, but does not authorize one definite elucidation as the only possible, or the most probable, interpretation.

1 Samuel 20 is akin to 1 Samuel 17, the David and Goliath story. Both are comparatively long and detailed. They both follow sections that are obscure, that leave a lot unsaid, and both offer a great deal of information that should clarify important points in the narrative, but both end with undecidable significance. In 1 Samuel 17, there is a duel in which only one will win, there will be a definitive outcome, but there are two outcomes, and the identity of one of the antagonists is not certain. The combat is a major event which ends indeterminately and which has no explicit significance for the continuing narrative. In 1 Samuel 20 there are lengthy speeches which should define motivations, purposes, and themes and thereby clarify some of the preceding problems and set the stage for the ongoing narrative. But not so. Jonathan will only appear once more after 1 Samuel 20 as an active character in the narrative before his death in 1 Samuel 31. David's opinion of him and of his covenant with him is not given, nor is any assessment made of the possible effects of the covenant on David's future.

The reading of 1 Samuel 20 will be similar to that of 1 Samuel 17 in terms of length, complexity, and the use of parallel material, but will be different because of the extensive dialogue and because there is now more background for the plot and the characters. In 1 Samuel 17, only Saul had extensive background; David had just been introduced in the preceding chapter, and Goliath appeared for the first time in 1 Samuel 17. 1 Samuel 20 involves three characters, David, Jonathan, and Saul, all of whom have been portrayed at some length in the previous narrative of 1 Samuel. Since I have already dealt in some detail with David and Saul and some of the possible relationships between them, I will not discuss them to the same extent that I will Jonathan; I have said little of him to this point. As with David and Saul, I will present alternate views of Jonathan's character, and I reiterate that the views are on a continuum and that most of the individual aspects making up a given "portrayal" are also on a continuum. When I list alternative interpretations of a given statement, act, or such, seldom are they necessarily mutually exclusive. I am not presenting a limited set of options that are each lucidly and separately defined. I also refer to, but do not enlarge upon, how the various options relate to the different views that each character can have of the others.

Before advancing to a reading of the narrative in 1 Samuel 20, I will briefly review the previous material on Jonathan for background on him as a character and on his relationships with Saul and David. The first reference to Jonathan is in the narrative of a military feat:

> Jonathan defeated the garrison [or, killed the governor] of the Philistines in Geba; and the Philistines heard of it. And Saul blew the trumpet throughout all the land, saying, "Let the Hebrews hear." And all Israel heard it said that Saul had defeated the garrison [or, killed the governor] of the Philistines. (1 Sam 13:3–4)

For whatever purpose, Saul is credited with the military feat, and there is possibly present a reason for Jonathan to resent Saul. The next two reports of Jonathan are neutral on this possibility since they note that Saul and Jonathan stayed together (13:16) and that, of all the army, only Saul and Jonathan had swords (13:22).

1 Samuel 14 and 20 are the two lengthiest narratives of Jonathan. In the battle of Michmash in 1 Samuel 14, Jonathan is portrayed as a capable warrior who threatens and then defeats a Philistine garrison accompanied only by his armor-bearer. Further, Jonathan attacks the garrison without telling his father or the rest of the army (14:1 and 3). This act can be understood as bravery, foolhardiness, and arrogance. Before actually challenging the garrison, Jonathan speaks to his armor-bearer and places the

ensuing conflict in a religious framework, "it may be that the Lord
will work for us; for nothing can hinder the Lord from saving by
many or by few" (14:6). As with David's proclamation to Goliath, it
is not certain whether Jonathan is sincere or is perhaps only trying
to encourage his young armor-bearer. Although the following defeat
of the Philistines by Saul and the army is ascribed to the Lord, "and
the Lord delivered Israel that day" (14:23), the actual slaughter of
the Philistine garrison is not explicitly ascribed to the Lord, but only
to Jonathan and his armor-bearer.

Jonathan does not leave the issue with just a proclamation of
the Lord's power, but proposes a sign that will reveal whether or
not the Lord will be with them in battle:

> Then said Jonathan, "Behold, we will cross over to the men,
> and we will show ourselves to them. If they say to us, 'Wait
> until we come to you,' then we will stand still in our place,
> and we will not go up to them. But if they say, 'Come up to
> us,' then we will go up; for the Lord has given them into
> our hand. And this shall be the sign for us." (14:8-10)

The latter occurs:

> And the men of the garrison hailed Jonathan and his
> armor-bearer, and said, "Come up to us, and we will show
> you a thing." And Jonathan said to his armor-bearer,
> "Come up after me; for the Lord has given them into the
> hand of Israel." (14:12)

The question of Jonathan's intention arises since the sign can be
understood as only a common sense proposal and not a test of the
divine will. That is, it is unlikely that the Philistine garrison would
come down to Jonathan and his armor-bearer because they would
fear an ambush, and the rocky crags on which they were perched
would prevent any surprise attack on the garrison if they remained
in their place. Finally, Jonathan would be aware of what the Philistine's response will be, and thus this would not be a true "sign," yet
the text leaves it open whether Jonathan is actually aware of this or
not.

If he does not know, then this is best regarded as a serious and
pious proposal on which their next move hinges. Moreover, this
understanding of the proposal is possible even if Jonathan is certain
of the Philistines' reply. On the other hand, given the certainty of
their reply, it could be just a ploy to bolster his armor-bearer; Jonathan later points out to him explicitly that the sign has been fulfilled

positively. Jonathan would be not only a formidable warrior, but also a good judge of people. Finally, the proposal could be merely a demonstration that Jonathan has a flair for the dramatic, a penchant for doing things with ceremony and show. The three expositions of the proposal can be taken as mutually exclusive, or two or all three can be combined in various ways into more complicated views of Jonathan's character. The text supports the wide range of possibilities, but does not authorize one of them or some particular combination of them.

In the midst of the ensuing battle, Saul pronounces an oath that is binding on the army; "Cursed be the man who eats food until it is evening and I am avenged on my enemies" (14:24). Jonathan, who has not heard his father's oath, eats some honey with "the tip of the staff that was in his hand" (14:27). A soldier immediately informs him of Saul's oath and Jonathan replies in strong terms.

> My father has troubled the land; see how my eyes have become bright, because I tasted a little of this honey. How much better if the army had eaten freely today of the spoil of the enemies which they found; for now the slaughter among the Philistines has not been great. (14:29–30)

Saul builds an altar to prevent the army from eating meat with the blood still in it and proposes that they, now refreshed, pursue the Philistines. A priest speaks up, "Let us draw near hither to God." Saul inquires of the Lord, "but he did not answer him that day" (14:36–37). No reason is given for the Lord's refusal to answer Saul, but Saul quickly provides his own explanation: "Come hither, all you leaders of the army; and know and see how this sin has arisen today" (14:38); some sin has been committed in Saul's opinion. Then, in a demonstration of religious fervor or of his own dramatic flair, Saul proclaims, "For as the Lord lives who saves Israel, though it be in Jonathan my son, he shall surely die" (14:39). This time, not even a soldier answers him since many, if not all, of them are probably aware that Jonathan ate the honey and thereby violated Saul's oath. Saul then proposes a lot casting procedure to choose between the army on one side and him and Jonathan on the other. Saul and Jonathan are taken, and next Jonathan is taken.

What, exactly, is happening here? The narrative leaves many points open. Why does Saul assume that "this sin" has been committed because the Lord does not respond to his inquiry? In the story in 1 Samuel 28, he does not make such an assumption, but goes to consult with the medium at Endor. Perhaps at this time, near the end of his life, he is in extremities that he is not in in 1 Samuel 14. When Saul says "this sin," does he have some particular transgression in mind, especially one related to his previous oath? If so, he does not say it explicitly. Why does he not relate "this sin" to the army's eating flesh with the blood in it? Why does he not just ask the army what possible sin or sins have been committed? If Saul has a specific sin in mind, the lot casting could then be superfluous. Finally, why does Jonathan's name come so readily to his lips in his initial response?

Saul's casting of lots can be appreciated as a formal and sacred affair, as an attempt to identify and then eradicate sin from within Israel. A similar procedure was used by Joshua to detect Achan who broke the ban placed on Jericho, and Achan had "brought trouble on Israel" (Joshua 7). On the other hand, the procedure can be perceived as the overreaction of Saul, as melodrama, or in a related vein, as a dramatic act to cover up his earlier blunders, especially his oath. The parallel with Achan's trial highlights the melodramatic aspect of the "trial" of Jonathan. The battle of Michmash was not a holy war declared by the Lord himself (see Josh 6:1–5), and Jonathan did not, like Achan (Josh 7:1 and 20–21), deliberately and secretly take silver and gold in violation of the divine ban, but unwittingly and publicly "tasted a little honey with the tip of [his] staff" in violation of his father's oath. And it is Saul, not Jonathan, who is accused of "troubling the land" (see Josh 7:25–26).

Once Jonathan has been taken by lot, Saul asks him, "Tell me what you have done." Jonathan replies, "I tasted a little honey with the tip of the staff that was in my hand; here I am, I will die" (14:43). Is this a pious Jonathan who will accept his father's decision whether it is wise or not? Or is this the more astute Jonathan who, by his statement, brings the issue to a brutal climax, thereby forcing the army to step in to prevent his father's serious blunder? Or is he to be discerned as a confident and somewhat arrogant Jonathan who defies and perhaps even scorns his father, knowing that the army will rescue him? In any case, there is now even more reason for Jonathan to resent and to be angered at Saul. Not only has Saul condemned him to death for eating a little honey, but he has also ignored his defeat of the garrison, a marvelous act that initiated the defeat of the Philistine army. The Israelite army does not ignore the feat: "Shall Jonathan die who has wrought this great victory in Israel . . . he has wrought with God this day" (14:45).

The next appearance of Jonathan in the narrative is in 1 Sam

18:1-4, the covenant with David which has been discussed from another viewpoint (81; 84). The covenant entails Jonathan's gift of his robe and armor to David. The brief episode is a manifestation only of Jonathan's affection and friendship for David, but given the preceding narratives which include Jonathan, it is also a manifestation of Jonathan's resentment of his father. The latter portrayal is supported by the statement in 18:1 that Jonathan was knit or bound to David since the verb "to knit, bind" (Heb.: *qšr*) is elsewhere best translated "to conspire" (see 1 Sam 22:8, 13). The portrayal does not have to exclude the friendship with David.

1 Sam 19:1-7 also was discussed previously and associated with 1 Samuel 14 (95-98). The reading of 1 Sam 19:1-7 can be expanded in light of the preceding analysis of 1 Samuel 14. In my earlier reading, I raised the question of what, in Jonathan's speech to him, made Saul take his oath not to kill David, and I suggested that it was "some subtle reminder of the possible consequences of such a violent deed as killing David" (97). I now add that the subtle reminder can work by allusion to Saul's near execution of Jonathan since that incident also entails talk of sin and great victory wrought with the Lord. Jonathan is attempting to shame his father into a reconciliation with David by reminding him of his previous blunder.

1 Samuel 20: David, Jonathan, and Saul: A Spear Thrown and an Arrow Shot

We come to the reading of the meeting between David and Jonathan with a range of possibilities for the characters of both David and Jonathan. In the case of Jonathan, the range extends from a pious and confident warrior who is loyal to his father in any situation and who is also a very close and loyal friend of David. The two loyalties, to father and to friend, can frequently leave Jonathan in a personal conflict. At the other end of the scale is a proud and arrogant warrior who is using his friendship with David, whether sincere or not, to avenge the past outrages inflicted upon him by Saul.

Saul's third attempt to kill David with his spear and his subsequent attempt to have him killed in his own house convinced David of Saul's murderous intent so that "he fled and escaped." David comes to Jonathan with no doubt that Saul is determined to put him to death, and his opening questions to Jonathan lead us to believe that he is now wondering why Saul is pursuing him. "What have I done? What is my guilt? And what is my sin before your father, that he seeks my life?" (20:1). Soon David reiterates his conviction, "truly, as the Lord lives and as you live, there is but a step between me and death" (20:3)/11/. However, despite David's flight and escape, it is still the case that he "should not fail to sit at table with the king" during the coming new moon festival (20:5). Does this duty reflect some type of reconciliation? Did something happen at Ramah to alter the relationship between him and David? Or is it that the break between the two is not yet total, that David for whatever reason will still appear at court, at least for major festivals?

David refers to "my guilt" and "my sin." Jonathan previously talked of sin in the context of Saul's attempt to kill David (19:1-7), and I noted that the issue is not developed in that context. Nor is it here. There is no talk in 1 Samuel 20 of wrong, sin, guilt, etc., regardless of whether they are understood in a moral, religious sense or in a political sense. There is no answer given to David's first question, "What have I done?"

As with most of David's "questions," the status of his questions to Jonathan is indeterminate. Are these literal questions? David is seriously asking what he has done wrong, morally, religiously, and politically, that has incurred Saul's wrath and his attempts to kill him; he is fully cognizant of Saul's resolve, but cannot understand why Saul is so determined. On the other hand, David is not concerned with anything that he has done, but is asking Jonathan what Saul has said are his reasons for trying to kill David. This posits a more cunning David. A third possibility will be mentioned later. Or are these rhetorical questions which would void the other possible readings? David is forcefully asserting that he has done nothing wrong nor in any way been disloyal to Saul that Saul should be seeking his life. Thus David is asking nothing of Jonathan.

David's response to Eliab's rebuke, "What have I done now?" (17:29), has already been discussed. David will ask analogous questions of Saul in 1 Sam 26:1 and of Achish of Gath in 1 Sam 29:8. The status of these three "questions" is also undecidable, although in the latter instance, there is good reason to read David's speech ironically. When Achish tells David that he cannot go to battle with him against Saul because of the objections of the Philistine generals, David replies, "But what have I done . . . that I may not go and fight against the enemies of my lord the king"? (29:8). "My lord the king": is this Achish or Saul? And if it is Achish, David has shown himself capable of lying to him and perhaps even of planning treachery against him. David raids distant peoples and tells Achish that he has attacked nearby groups in the Negeb; he massacres all the people attacked so that no one will tell Achish what David has done (1 Sam 27:8–12). Such deceit, if known, would provide Achish with good reason for not trusting David in a battle with Israel.

The parallels cannot decide the issue of the status of David's "questions." Nor does Jonathan's response, in which he apparently expresses ignorance of his father's determination and buttresses the claim by stating that his father would assuredly tell him of such a resolve. "Far from it! You shall not die. Behold, my father does nothing either great or small without disclosing it to me; and why should my father hide this from me? It is not so" (20:2). It is difficult, if not impossible, to understand how Jonathan could not know or believe that Saul is resolved to eliminate David. Saul has told him so specifically, and Jonathan has expressed his knowledge to David: "Saul my father seeks to kill you" (19:1–2). In 1 Samuel 14 Jonathan himself came close to dying at his father's command; he should have no doubt about that of which Saul is capable. The prophesying at Ramah may have so changed Jonathan's opinion of his father that David's statement now shocks him. Yet, as already indicated, the event has not had this effect on David.

On the other hand, Jonathan knows what his father plans, but does not or cannot believe that Saul is so strongly resolved that he will actually kill David, or that he is so strongly resolved that there is no hope for reconciliation between David and Saul. Jonathan is torn by his conflicting loyalties to the two men. Thus he goes along with David in the meeting with the hope that Saul will not be angered at David's absence from the feast. In another alternative portrayal, Jonathan knows what his father plans against David and is angered by it. His anger is increased by his resentment of his father's past abuses of himself. Jonathan thereby goes along with David in the meeting hoping to find some opportunity for revenge against Saul. The latter two scenarios regard Jonathan's statements about Saul's determination and his communication of it to David as a pretext for other, as yet unexpressed, concerns. The possibility will be traced through the remainder of the chapter.

Before continuing with the reading of the opening conversation, I want to jump ahead to a verse which speaks specifically about Jonathan's knowledge: "And Saul cast his spear at him [Jonathan] to smite him; and Jonathan knew that his father was determined to put David to death" (20:33). Is there a causal relation between the casting of the spear and Jonathan's knowledge, or are these two independent statements of the text presented in metonymic order? The text supports both interpretations at the same time. The first alternative, the causal relation, allows a wide range for the extent of Jonathan's previous ignorance, from near total to the hope that he might be wrong. The effect of the spear cast accordingly extends from a sudden, unexpected knowledge of his father's hostility, to confirmation of what he had known . or suspected, and to an awareness of the depth of the hostility towards David. The latter is the reading in McCarter's translation of vs. 33, "But when Saul raised his spear against him to strike him, [he] realized that his father was so intent upon evil that he would kill David" (334). The range of expositions of vs. 33 allows a similar wide range of interpretations of the initial meeting and conversation between David and Jonathan.

On the contrary, the two clauses in vs. 33 may be independent and not related by necessity or time. This is to say, Saul cast his spear at that moment, and Jonathan knew of his father's determination from some time before the incident and perhaps even before the meeting with David. In the upcoming reading of the story of Ahimelech of Nob in 1 Samuel 21–22, I provide some specific examples of the narrative technique of supplying information relevant to a particular episode or narrative later in the narrative than would be expected or even after the narrative has been concluded. The technique is a type of "flashback" and is the opposite of anticipation. An example, within a character's speech, is Jonathan's statement that Saul saw David kill Goliath and rejoiced (19:5). This, 20:33, is an example of the technique in the narration itself. Taking it as such an example supports the scenario that Jonathan is outraged by his father's previous actions against himself and against David and is seeking some form of revenge. It also upholds the corollary that knowledge of Saul's intentions and plans is not the issue for Jonathan since he has a clear idea of what Saul is about and why. I return now to the opening scene between David and Jonathan.

Jonathan's response to David's first "questions" begins, "Far from it! You shall not die." This is reminiscent of Saul's previous oath to Jonathan, "As the Lord lives, he [David] shall not be put to death" (19:6); Jonathan is recalling it specifically and assuring David that it is still in effect, that Saul's hostility is not so intense that he will go so far as to kill David. On the other hand, granted that

Jonathan knows and believes Saul's resolve to kill David, this is an assertion that no harm will come to David, similar to that made by him in 1 Sam 23:17—"Fear not; for the hand of Saul my father shall not find you"—and not a denial that Saul seeks David's life.

"My father does nothing either great or small without disclosing it to me; and why should my father hide this from me? It is not so." The statement provides strong support for the interpretation that Jonathan does not know or does not believe that Saul has already reneged on his promise to him and has tried to kill David at least twice. Therefore, there is no reason for him to respond to David's "questions" about what he has done to incur Saul's wrath.

As an alternative, to interpret the statement with the assumption of Jonathan's full knowledge of his father's determination is to regard Jonathan as lying outright or as, in some manner, prevaricating. Later in the chapter, Jonathan will have no qualms about lying to Saul about David's absence. Or Jonathan may just be evading David's questions, waffling on the issue, since he says nothing about what David has done or about any guilt or sin.

"Why should my father hide this from me? It is not so." What is not so? That Saul seeks David's life, or that Saul has hidden his intentions from Jonathan? Soon Jonathan will again "ask" David, "If I knew that it was determined by my father that evil should come upon you, would I not tell you?" (20:9). As with so many of the "questions" that we have encountered, this is an assertion that Jonathan will certainly tell David, or a serious question that can be answered in the negative. Jonathan is aware of his father's plans, but will not yet reveal them to David.

David "swore again" (20:3); the chapter is marked by oaths, covenants, and oath formulas. David does not ask his "questions" again even though Jonathan has not answered them. Instead, he responds directly to Jonathan's assertion that his father tells him everything. "Your father knows well that I have found favor in your eyes; and he thinks, 'Let not Jonathan know this, lest he be grieved'" (20:3). He then reiterates that Saul is intent on killing him, "But truly, as the Lord lives and as you live, there is but a step between me and death." (David's response foreshadows the statement that Jonathan "was grieved for David, because his father had humiliated him" [20:34].) Finally, it can be assumed that, whatever Jonathan may know or believe of Saul, he by now knows that David is convinced that Saul is determined to kill him.

"Then said Jonathan to David, 'Whatever you say, I will do for you'" (20:4). Jonathan sidesteps the issue of Saul's determination, and he has apparently been reading between the lines since David has said nothing about Jonathan doing something for him. Or Jonathan is responding to David's opening "questions" as asking about Saul's plans and purposes, i.e., as asking Jonathan to spy for him. Whether or not it is in accord with his original purpose, David goes along with Jonathan's offer and proposes a plan that is similar to the one proposed by Jonathan in 19:2–3 except that David's is more elaborate. The plan may have been concocted by David on the spur of the moment, and therefore he follows a familiar course of action. Above I suggested a similar interpretation of David who responded spontaneously to Saul's requirement of 100 Philistine foreskins as a marriage present for Michal (86). Here, with Jonathan, David is again demonstrating that he is a "man prudent in speech." Finally, from David's viewpoint his plan accords with the conviction that Saul is set on killing him; his absence from the festival denies Saul an opportunity to do so.

David explains the first part of his plan to Jonathan. He will hide "in the field" until the third day of the new moon festival. During the festival, David "should not fail to sit at the table with the king." If he is missed by Saul, David provides Jonathan with an excuse: "If your father misses me at all, then say, 'David earnestly asked leave of me to run to Bethlehem his city; for there is a yearly sacrifice there for all the family'" (20:6). It is this excuse which is the key to David's plan. "If he [Saul] says, 'Good!' it will be well with your servant; but if he is angry, then know that evil is determined by him" (20:7). In the speech David has shifted from "I" and "me" to the formal "your servant." This is reminiscent of his proclamations to Saul in 1 Sam 17:32–37, and here it probably reflects an appeal to the covenant between David and Jonathan which is mentioned in the next verse, "for you have brought your servant into a covenant of the Lord" (20:8). David uses the phrase "your servant" two more times in his speech and then goes back to "I" and "me." David's plan corresponds to the assumption that he knows full well what Saul's reaction will be. He says to Jonathan, "if he is angry, *then know* that evil is determined by him." It is Jonathan's knowledge, not his own, that he wants to establish or confirm.

Having explained the plan, David concludes by admonishing Jonathan, in very weighty terms, to "deal kindly [or, loyally] with your servant, for you have brought your servant into a *covenant of the Lord* with you" (20:8). The previous mention of a formal agreement between David and Jonathan was of a covenant without the sacral overtones of the phrase "of the Lord": "Jonathan made a covenant with David" (18:3). David returns to the theme of guilt that was introduced in the opening conversation. "But if there is guilt in me, slay me yourself; for why should you bring me to your father?" (20:8). Again the problem of the status of the "question." A rhetorical question: an assertion that there is no reason for Jonathan to harm David or turn him over to Saul, and David does not fear that Jonathan will do so. A literal question: evidently David does not trust Jonathan for some reason; he fears that he will betray him and even turn him over to Saul. However, McCarter's translation of the statement lessens the fear, "If there were any guilt in me, you could kill me yourself! So why should you turn me over to your father?" (332).

The admonishment of Jonathan raises the question of David's purpose in coming to him. Is it a concern with Saul and his plans, or is it a concern with Jonathan and what he knows and is going to do? David wants Jonathan to be convinced thoroughly of Saul's intentions and plans so that Jonathan will not turn against him.

"A covenant of the Lord": in his admonishment of Jonathan, David adds the sacral element "of the Lord" which was not mentioned in 18:3. Is David referring to a sacred covenant between himself and Jonathan that has not been reported in the narrative? This is McCarter's understanding: "Our narrator has not mentioned this sacred agreement before, but it was an important part of the tradition and described in 18:1–5" (341). On the other hand, there is no such sacred agreement, and David is adding the phrase to increase the seriousness of the covenant and, consequently, of any breach of it by Jonathan. The latter construal accords with the use of the formal phrase, "your servant," and as McCarter notes, David's request that Jonathan "deal kindly or loyally" with him means "to act in accordance with *ḥésed* (fidelity to an agreement . . .)" (341).

There is a parallel to such a ploy in Genesis 27, a narrative entailing a father, sons, a meal, and deception. Isaac tells Esau to prepare a meal for him "that I may bless you before I die" (27:4). Rebekah overhears the conversation and repeats it to Jacob, her favorite son, with an addition to make the proposed blessing more serious which should help overcome her son's reluctance to engage in the deception she has planned. Rebekah reports the latter part of Isaac's speech, "[that I may] bless you *before the Lord* before I die" (27:7).

David's statement, "But if there is guilt in me, slay me yourself; for why should you bring me to your father," is paralled by Absalom's demand of Joab, "Now therefore let me go into the presence of the king; and if there is guilt in me, let him kill me" (2 Sam 14:32). The situation in 2 Samuel entails another trio: King David, Absalom his son, and Joab his army commander; I briefly discussed such "trios" above (95). Absalom's demand of Joab is preceded by the narrative of his flight because of his murder of Amnon (2 Samuel 13) and by Joab's intercession with David to obtain permission for Absalom to return to Jerusalem (2 Sam 14:1-24). The intercession is undertaken by Joab when he "perceived that the king's heart went out to Absalom" (14:1) and probably concluded that the king's emotional concern would interfere with his ruling effectively. Later Joab stresses that David's emotional reaction to Absalom's death, if not contained, will result in loss of the people's loyalty (2 Sam 19:1-9).

The episode in 2 Samuel 14 is also related to that in 1 Sam 19:1-7 although there are shifts in the roles of the "characters." In the latter the son, Jonathan, intercedes on his own initiative with his father the king for the return of David, the army commander, because Jonathan "delighted much in David" (1 Sam 19:1). David "was in [Saul's] presence as before" (1 Sam 19:7); Absalom returns to Jerusalem, but "did not see the king's face" (2 Sam 14:24). Absalom goes to Joab and demands just this, to go into the presence of the king, in the passage cited above.

After living apart for two years, Absalom finally comes into the king's presence, but soon "got himself a chariot and horses, and fifty men to run before him" (2 Sam 15:1). He sits as a judge in the gate for "all of Israel who came to the king for judgment" and thereby "Absalom stole the hearts of the men of Israel" (15:6). Does David have some analogous purpose in mind when he comes to Jonathan? Are his plans more long range than just Saul's and Jonathan's immediate plans and intentions? Are his eyes on eventual kingship? Absalom certainly did not act impetuously, but could wait years before carrying out a plan. Two years went by between Amnon's rape of Tamar and his murder by Absalom (2 Sam 13:23), and Absalom dwelt in Geshur for three years before returning to Jerusalem (13:38). This adds another possible David to those listed above, a David suggested by the parallel with his residence with Achish of Gath (1 Samuel 27 and 29).

The issues raised by these parallels with the Absalom story will be further developed at a later point in the reading and will be augmented by viewing, as parallel characters, Jonathan and Absalom and not just David and Absalom. Further attention will be given to the different motivations for interceding with the king for the return of the other person: concern for the king and the kingdom, and personal loyalty and friendship.

To return to 1 Samuel 20, Jonathan's response to David's admonishment is assuring, but it does not address David's fear that Jonathan will hand him over to Saul; it avoids a direct response. "Far be it from you! If I knew that it was determined by my father that evil should come upon you, would I not tell you?" (20:9). The undecidability of the status of the "question" was stressed above (109).

Although David has twice unequivocally asserted that Saul seeks to kill him and has only asked Jonathan to find out and to tell him why, David replies directly to Jonathan's assurance by asking, "Who will tell me if your father answers you roughly?" (20:10). David knows well how Saul will answer Jonathan. However, the question to Jonathan does fit with David's interest in Jonathan's knowledge, i.e., how will I know that you are convinced that your father is trying to kill me?

On the other hand, the question also fits with David's longer range plans eventually to supplant Saul as king. In this explication of the story, David comes to Jonathan with no specific plans in mind, but to see how he might "use" Jonathan and his friendship and covenant with him to further his own designs on the kingship. Therefore David responds directly to each of Jonathan's statements, hoping that some specific advantage for himself will reveal itself. At this point, 20:9–10, David senses that Jonathan can be an effective, although unwitting, spy for him.

The conversation continues characteristically since Jonathan does not answer David's question immediately. "And Jonathan said to David, 'Come, let us go out into the field.' So they both went out into the field" (20:11). (Future reading will have to assess the significance of the detail of going into the field.) Once in the field, Jonathan reiterates, more elaborately, the assurance he gave David a short time before that he will tell him Saul's reaction to the "excuse" for David's absence from the royal table. He still does not directly address David's specific concern, "Who will tell me . . . ?"

> When I have sounded my father, about this time tomorrow, or the third day, behold, if he is well disposed toward

> David, shall I not then send and disclose it to you? But
> should it please my father to do you harm, the Lord do so
> to Jonathan, and more also, if I do not disclose it to you,
> and send you away, that you may go in safety. May the
> Lord be with you, as he has been with my father.
> (20:12–13)

"May the Lord be with you, as he has been with my father." Given
the disastrous effects of the Spirit of the Lord on Saul in previous
incidents, does Jonathan realize the ironic significance of his wish
(see 16:14–23; 18:10–11; 19:9–10; and perhaps 19:23–24)?

Jonathan still does not give any specifics as to how he will
inform David; instead he involves him in another oath. The Hebrew
text of 20:14–16 is possibly troubled, and the precise reading is not
sure. Jonathan does pick up on David's previous admonishment to
deal with him kindly or loyally and similarly uses the weighty "of
the Lord," but now relates it to David's actions toward himself and
toward his house, his descendants. Three times Jonathan speaks of
something being "cut off" which hearkens back to the David and
Goliath story and associated passages and to the violence that the
phrase connotes, the violence which is never far from a reading of
the story of David (see above: 81–82). Jonathan is willing to help
David against his father, but he also apparently fears that David
may betray him, that he may be using him for the moment and will
turn against him in the future when he is in a less precarious situation. I also note, but do not trace, the theme of dynasty and dynastic succession introduced in Jonathan's reference to his house.

Jonathan's purposes, however they may or may not involve
Saul, are directed toward getting David to swear to the proposed
oath. When they meet, each responds to the other's statements, not
to answer them directly, but to ascertain if there is some way each
can lead the other to the position that he wants him in. Such
possible interpretations, however, lead us, as readers, into the situation encountered in the David and Goliath story. It is not just the
reader's view of David that is open, but also of Jonathan. Added to
this are David's view of Jonathan and Jonathan's view of David,
views which may or may not correspond to the reader's views of
David and Jonathan.

"Jonathan made David swear by his love for him; for he loved
him as he loved himself" (20:17). Jonathan loves David, and David
loves Jonathan. David, to attain his purposes whatever they are,
must take an oath to guarantee the safety of Jonathan and his

house. "He loved him as he loved himself" does not prevent either Jonathan or David from trying to manipulate the other for his own ends. Again, Saul and his plans are not the issue between David and Jonathan.

Jonathan proposes a complicated sign for David which entails shooting three arrows and then sending his lad after them. David will know Saul's reaction by the directions that Jonathan gives to the lad. In the defeat of the Philistine garrison at Michmash in 1 Samuel 14, Jonathan evinced a similar predilection for acted-out signs when he proposed a sign to his young armor-bearer that the Lord would or would not give them victory over the garrison (see above: 102–3). The proposal to David is in character and is suscepti- ble to a wide range of interpretation which extends from a serious attempt to communicate publicly, yet secretly, with David to an attempt to impress David with Jonathan's sincerity and trustworthi- ness so that David will be more apt to keep any covenant made with Jonathan. The proposal could also be just a manifestation of Jonathan's flair for the dramatic, his penchant for doing things with hidden and secret meanings.

Jonathan closes his proposal by reminding David of the previ- ous oath and by reemphasizing its seriousness. "As for the matter of which you and I have spoken, behold, the Lord is between you and me for ever" (20:23). Twice Jonathan has ended a speech to David with reference to this oath. The oath, and not Saul, is Jonathan's concern.

The conversation between David and Jonathan ends with Jona- than's reminder, and narration begins, but it is soon broken by more dialogue. David hides himself and is missed by Saul at the new moon meal. Saul says nothing on the first day, thinking that David is not ritually clean, but on the second day, he does ask Jonathan where "the son of Jesse" has been for the first two days of the festival (20:27). Jonathan replies by quoting the excuse that David gave him earlier concerning the family sacrifice in Bethlehem and embellishes it by adding to David's speech: "my brother has commanded me to be there. So now, if I have found favor in your eyes, let me get away, and see my brothers" (20:29). We can speculate why Jonathan made the addition and what could be the significance and the effect on Saul of the references to David's brother and brothers. There is an allusion back to his clash with Eliab in 17:28–29 and forward to his "escape" to the cave of Adullam where "his brothers and all his father's house" joined him (1 Sam 22:1). Jonathan's embellishment can have a positive impact on Saul by stressing that David has been "commanded" to attend the family sacrifice. Finally, does Jonathan realize the irony of the phrase "let me get away" which can also be translated "let me escape" (Heb.: *mlṭ*)?

Saul's response to the proferred excuse is anger, but against Jonathan, not David.

> Then Saul's anger was kindled against Jonathan, and he said to him, "You son of a perverse, rebellious woman, do I not know that you have chosen the son of Jesse to your own shame, and to the shame of your mother's nakedness?" (20:30)

Saul appends a reason why Jonathan's choice of David is so shameful: "As long as the son of Jesse lives upon the earth, neither you nor your kingdom shall be established" (20:31). Not Saul's kingdom, but Jonathan's. Saul is appealing to Jonathan's self-interest so that he will bring David to him to be put to death: "Therefore, send and fetch him to me, for he shall surely die" (20:31). Jonathan, however, has already attempted to serve his own interests through his dealings with David, through his covenant with him, and not by handing him over to Saul, "for he loved him as he loved himself."

On the other hand, Jonathan is Saul's son and if his kingdom will not be established, then neither will Saul's. Thus Saul has provided a partial answer to Jonathan's "questions" which echo David's from the opening of the chapter. "Why should he be put to death? What has he done" (20:32). Saul is convinced that, if he lives, David will ultimately replace him as king of Israel. What is not stated is why Saul thinks this and whether he thinks that David is actively plotting against him to become king; nothing is said of anything David has done, of any sin or guilt, whether religious or political.

Saul's rejoinder to Jonathan's questions about David is an attempt to kill him with his spear as he had tried three times before with David.

> And Saul cast his spear at him to smite him; and Jonathan knew that his father was determined to put David to death. And Jonathan rose from the table in fierce anger and ate no food the second day of the month, for he was grieved for David, for his father had disgraced him. (20:33–34)

I have already indicated that Jonathan's grief was foreshadowed in a statement by David in vs. 3, and I discussed at some length the problem of the possible relationships of the first two clauses in the quotation (above, 107–8).

Vs. 34 is striking in its combination of literal clarity and obscure significance. "Jonathan rose from the table in fierce anger and ate no food the second day of the month." The statement is straightforward, but what precisely is it saying, and how does it relate to the context? It may or may not have anything to do with the spear cast and with Jonathan's knowledge of Saul's determination. Vs. 25 reports a similar action of Jonathan's while at table, "and Jonathan rose," but with no hint of the significance or purpose of the act/12/. In neither vs. 25 nor vs. 34 does the rising lead to leaving or any other positive action; apparently Jonathan remains at table, but standing and not sitting. Saul's spear cast at Jonathan thereby has a parallel since David evades Saul's spear throw twice, but does not leave the royal court because of it (18:10–11).

Jonathan's not eating—is he fasting?—stands in inverted relationship with his eating honey in violation of Saul's curse in 1 Samuel 14. Both episodes entail Saul's attempting to kill Jonathan, and both include the use of some system of signs, lot casting or arrows, to gain or impart decisive information. Both systems of signs are serious endeavors, or melodramatic displays, or attempts to impress and influence others. Finally, Jonathan's "fierce anger" can be the result of the spear cast, or it can be only the expression of his rage which goes back to the honey incident and even further back to Saul's being credited with Jonathan's military feat against the Philistines in 1 Sam 13:1–4. The motives for the anger can also be combined in various ways.

The text provides motivation for Jonathan's anger and not eating: "for he was grieved for David, for his father had disgraced him." Some aspects of the text remain open. First is the issue of Jonathan's grief (Heb.: '*ṣb*). Is it akin to David's grief over his dead son Absalom: "the people heard that day, 'The king is *grieving* [Heb.: *ne'e̊ṣab*] for his son'" (2 Sam 19:3)? Or is it akin to David's not bothering or displeasing his son Adonijah: "His father had never at any time *displeased* [Heb.: *lō' 'åṣābô*] him by asking, 'Why have you done thus and so?'" (1 Kgs 1:6)? What is Jonathan's emotion, and how intense is it?

Second, did Saul disgrace David or Jonathan, and how did he disgrace him? If it is Jonathan, the humiliation, the disgrace, could derive from Saul's attempt on his life, from his realization, if we assume an ignorant Jonathan here, that Saul had hidden something so important from him, from Saul's attack on his mother—"You son of a perverse, rebellious woman"—or from one of the previous episodes involving Saul and Jonathan. If it is David, the disgrace could stem from Saul's firm resolution to kill David or from one of the earlier conflicts between Saul and David that Jonathan knows about.

Finally, the relation between the humiliation and the "grief" is not explicitly stated. If the humiliation is of David, it can then motivate the grief or concern for David: "Your father knows well that I have found favor in your eyes; and he thinks, 'Let not Jonathan know this, lest he be grieved'" (20:3). However, if Saul had disgraced Jonathan, then the humiliation is another motivation, in addition to the "grief," for Jonathan's anger and not eating. The latter interpretation leaves open why Jonathan is "grieved" for David. Shortly I will propose another way of accounting for the humiliation and the "grief."

The reading of this one verse is indeterminate since the verse sustains a spectrum of readings, some of which I have been tracing through the story of the meeting between David and Jonathan. In one range of interpretation, that which is found in most commentaries on the chapter, firm knowledge of Saul's determination to kill David is the essential issue, and the majority of the narrative is concerned with the gaining or the imparting of that information. Jonathan's arrow-shooting sign and his excuse for David's absence proffered to Saul are integral parts of the plan and are not motivated by reasons other than getting and giving the information. Jonathan's anger results from his realization, or the confirmation of his suspicions, that Saul is intent on killing David; he then informs David. However, most of the aspects of this type of exposition are themselves susceptible to a continuum of interpretation; we are not dealing with separate and distinct items which are to be systematically arranged into a "character portrayal." For example, I have already laid out some possible ranges for understanding the extent of Jonathan's knowledge of his father's plans from the start, of David's purposes in coming to Jonathan, especially in view of his admonishment of him, of Jonathan's reasons for making a covenant with David, and of the significance of Jonathan's "addition" of David's brothers to the excuse that he gives Saul.

Other possible readings of 1 Samuel 20, some of which I have been developing, are also susceptible to similar ranges of interpretations in their various aspects and elements. For example, if knowledge of Saul's intentions and motivations is not the main issue, then is such knowledge one issue among others, a secondary and minor issue, or only a pretext to cover other concerns? But what, then, are the other concerns, whether those of David or Jonathan? Both may fear some sort of betrayal by the other and are therefore attempting to get the other to swear to an oath or covenant that would lessen, if not remove, the chance of betrayal. Both David and Jonathan may be attempting to manipulate each other for their own self-interest, fearful or not. But, then, how do they regard each other? Do they respect or fear each other? What do they think that the other one wants and is trying to do? The possible answers and combinations are myriad.

Over and above what is occurring between David and Jonathan, there is the relationship between Jonathan and Saul. If Jonathan knows and is convinced of his father's resolve to kill David, then what has happened at the festival table? Jonathan is resentful and enraged toward his father for his past abuses against him and against David, and Jonathan is attempting to obtain some form of revenge for these. He is confident of his own capabilities, perhaps to the point of arrogance, and given to display and ceremony, to doing things not in a simple, straightforward manner, but in a complicated, oblique fashion. He comes to the royal table knowing well what Saul's reaction to the excuse for David's absence will be, and his statement of the excuse heavy with scorn and designed for negative effect to infuriate his father further. It is not David's father or whole family who have "commanded" him to leave Saul and come to the family sacrifice, but only one brother, and when has David ever paid attention to a brother? Saul's rage and attempt to kill him with his spear are foregone conclusions for Jonathan. His anger is the culmination of long smoldering frustration and resentment toward his father.

To aid in the expansion and complication of some of these particular construals of the text and to add others to them, I introduce Jonathan's last appearance in the narrative as an active character and will then return to the prior discussion of parallels with the revolt of Absalom narrative. Following the meeting between David and Jonathan narrated in 1 Samuel 20, Jonathan appears once more as an active character; he comes to encourage David during his flight from Saul.

> David saw that Saul had come out to seek his life. David was in the Wilderness of Ziph at Horesh. And Jonathan, Saul's son, rose, and went to David at Horesh, and strengthened his

> hand in God. And he said to him, "Fear not; for the hand of
> Saul my father shall not find you; you shall be king over
> Israel, and I shall be next to you [or, your second-in-
> command]; Saul my father also knows this." And the two of
> them made a covenant before the Lord; David remained at
> Horesh, and Jonathan went home. (1 Sam 23:15–18)

The entire text is intriguing, but I focus for my purposes on the
statement by Jonathan.

"Fear not!" The only time prior to this that the text speaks of
David's fear is in 21:13 when David is "much afraid of Achish the
king of Gath." There is no other mention before or after Jonathan's
assurance of David's being afraid of Saul. Jonathan's assurance "fear
not" is expressing the fact that David is indeed afraid of Saul,
although this is not stated elsewhere in the narrative; at the same
time it is only expressing Jonathan's belief that David fears Saul;
finally, and at the same time, it is only an appropriate introduction
to the rest of Jonathan's speech and expresses no facts or beliefs.
With the latter, the main point is not David's fears, but the next
assurance that "the hand of Saul my father shall not find you." This
is analogous to Jonathan's former assurance to David, "Far from it!
You shall not die" (20:2).

Faced with the ambiguity of Jonathan's assurance, "Fear not,"
and the lack of any other mention of David's fear of Saul, some
Bible translations, e.g., the *NAB* and the *RSV*, and some commentaries, e.g., Smith, Ackroyd, and McCarter, emend the first word of
vs. 15 to read "David was afraid" instead of "David saw." "This is
shown by v 17 to be the correct understanding" (McCarter, 374),
and "David's *fear* is the proper introduction to Jonathan's
consolation" (Smith, 213; his italics.) Both arguments have resolved
the ambiguity of Jonathan's "fear not" by unequivocally asserting
that David is afraid of Saul and that Jonathan knows it, and then
they rewrite the preceding text in light of their assertion.

"You shall be king over Israel" (*RSV*) or "You will rule over
Israel" (McCarter, 373). Is Jonathan expressing knowledge, belief, or
hope? Or is there some other reason for Jonathan to say this, a reason
that has nothing to do with whether David is going to be king or not?
"I shall be next to you" (*RSV*) or "I shall be your second-in-command"
(McCarter, 373). "[Jonathan] expects *nothing more* for himself than
the position of second-in-command" (McCarter, 375), and "[Jonathan]
himself *fades into the background*, like the 'friend of the
bridegroom' when the hour comes" (Hertzberg, 193). On the other

hand, Jonathan is pushing himself into the foreground by demanding a position of high authority, if not a position equal to that of David. The Hebrew term for "next to you" or "second-in-command" is *mishneh* and elsewhere means "second-in-command," e.g., 2 Kgs 23:4; 25:18; Jer 52:24; "second born," e.g., 1 Sam 8:2; 17:13; 2 Sam 3:3; also "double" and "copy," e.g., Gen 43:12; Exod 16:5, 22; Deut 17:18. Jonathan is second to David in command or birth and, at the same time, his double or copy, his equal.

"Saul my father also knows this," i.e., both David's future rule and Jonathan's being with him. Saul said as much to Jonathan at the new moon festival:

> Do I not know that you have chosen the son of Jesse to your own shame, and to the shame of your mother's nakedness? For as long as the son of Jesse lives upon the earth, neither you nor your kingdom shall be established. (20:30–31)

Second, Saul's accusation of the Benjaminites gathered at his court implies that Saul knows that David will or might become king, for who else can dispense land and military posts but the king? The charge against Jonathan is explicit and emphasizes Saul's knowledge.

> Hear now, you Benjaminites; will the son of Jesse give every one of you fields and vineyards, will he make all of you commanders of thousands and commanders of hundreds, that all of you have conspired against me? No one discloses to me when my son makes a league with the son of Jesse, none of you is sorry for me or discloses to me that my son has stirred up my servant against me, to lie in wait, as at this day. (1 Sam 22:7–8)

1 Sam 20:34 uses the two verbs, to grieve (Heb.: *ṣb*) and to disgrace (Heb.: *klm*). The only other place the two verbs occur in such close proximity is 2 Sam 19:3–4, David's reaction to the news of Absalom's death.

> So the victory that day was turned into mourning for all the people; for the people heard that day, "The king is *grieving* for his son." And the people stole into the city that day as people steal in who are *humiliated (disgraced)* when they flee in battle.

In the foregoing analysis, I indicated the ambiguity of Jonathan's grief in 20:34 in relation to David's grief in this passage (117), and now note that the disgrace in 2 Samuel 19 supports the understanding that

Saul's disgracing, whether David or Jonathan, involves an affront in the military area. In the 2 Samuel story, Joab realizes the disastrous consequences that can result from the situation and tells David,

> You have today covered with shame the faces of all your servants, who have this day saved your life . . . for today I perceive that if Absalom were alive and all of us were dead today, then you would be pleased. Now therefore arise, go out and speak kindly to your servants; for I swear by the Lord, if you do not go, not a man will stay with you this night; and this will be worse for you than all the evil that has come upon you from your youth until now. (2 Sam 19:6–8)

David responds by taking his seat in the gate, "and all the people came before the king" (19:10).

Joab is one of the main characters in the Absalom story. He perceives that the king is pining for Absalom and is instrumental in his return from exile in Geshur. Next, and at Absalom's own request, he has him returned to the king's presence. However, Absalom takes advantage of the position to set the stage for a rebellion against David. In the ensuing battle, Joab personally kills, or at least oversees the death of, the young man. He probably does this both because of the threat to the kingdom posed by a live Absalom and because Absalom had taken advantage of him earlier to launch his revolt. Finally, it is Joab who intervenes in the speech just cited with the distraught David to prevent him from losing all that he has just gained by not valuing the army's accomplishment.

Earlier I compared David and Absalom even though they occupy different positions vis-à-vis the king; in 1 Samuel David is the king's army commander while in 2 Samuel Absalom is the king's son. I now compare Jonathan, the king's son in 1 Samuel, with his counterpart in 2 Samuel, Absalom, and also with Joab, the king's army commander in 2 Samuel. The latter, Jonathan and Joab, is the reverse of the comparison between David and Absalom. The comparisons are possible because Jonathan is both royal son and army commander. The comparisons can be developed in many different directions, and I present an exposition of the scene at the royal table in 1 Samuel 20 that attributes to Jonathan aspects first of Joab and then of Absalom.

As mentioned above, one interpretation is that Jonathan is enraged at Saul because he has not valued his military accomplishments both by taking credit for them and by ignoring them. Thus

Saul is analogous to King David in 2 Samuel 19. Jonathan is concerned about David because Saul had humiliated him, Jonathan, and if he would do this to his son, then what would he not do to his army commander? His distress is increased since he realizes, as Joab does in 2 Samuel 19, that the king's emotion can have disastrous consequences for the king and the kingdom. Saul's obsessive behavior is alienating and turning against him his two most competent military leaders, Jonathan and David. Despite his anger and humiliation, Jonathan never deserts Saul and eventually dies with him in the battle on Mt. Gilboa. He stays with him because Saul is still his father and because he has the faint hope that he may somehow turn Saul back from the onrushing disaster. At the same time, he maintains his friendship with David because of his personal affection for him and to prevent David from entering into active rebellion against Saul. He is successful in the latter since David flees from Saul and never pursues him.

In an alternate scenario, Jonathan is concerned about David because Saul had humiliated him, David, and Jonathan fears what David might do in retaliation. Jonathan first tries to convince David that his father is not determined to kill David at all costs and then that, regardless of his father's determination, his father will not be able to capture him and kill him. Indeed, Jonathan goes so far as to assure David that he will be king of Israel and, by implication, that he does not have to engage in actual combat with Saul to achieve this because "Saul my father also knows this." This explication holds regardless of whether or not Jonathan believes that David will be king. Yet he does fear David's violent retaliation and, in that eventuality, attempts to assure that the destruction will not befall him and his house. Jonathan stays with Saul because he is his father and because he feels that that is the best position from which to forestall active hostilities between David and Saul.

These portrayals of Jonathan derive from parallels with Joab in 2 Samuel; parallels with Absalom yield more sinister portrayals. To compare Jonathan with Absalom adds a new range of color to the spectrum, a range of motivation which derives from the assumption that Jonathan has some specific desires of his own for the kingship and that he is taking some concrete steps to fulfill the desires. Again, I could play with varying intensities for his desires, with different plans and their degrees of explicitness, with sundry ways of implicating David in the schemes, and so on and so forth, but I restrict myself to another exposition of the royal table scene in 1 Samuel 20.

Jonathan wants to succeed Saul as king as soon as possible and will let little stand in his way; on the other hand, he is willing to wait for Saul's death whether by natural causes or in battle. He is enraged at Saul because Saul has not valued his military achievements, and this could easily hinder or even prevent his future succession to the throne. However, he is most deeply troubled by Saul's obsessive behavior, especially toward himself and toward David. Saul is alienating his two most competent military leaders during a time of continued warfare with the Philistines and is thereby endangering the stability and future of the entire kingdom. If Saul loses the kingdom, then Jonathan loses the kingdom. Jonathan is caught in the middle between Saul and David. He stays with Saul for this is still his best (and only?) chance at succession in the event of Saul's death; he gambles, but unlike David's gamble in his duel with Goliath, Jonathan loses. At the same time, Jonathan also fears David's retaliation against Saul, for if it were successful, David would certainly be the next king and not Jonathan. Jonathan thereby maintains his alliance and "friendship" with David to prevent violent retaliation against Saul and also to insure for himself some measure of power if and when David does become king.

I return now to the reading of 1 Samuel 20. "In the morning, Jonathan went out into the field to the appointment with David, and with him a little lad" (20:35). Jonathan carries through with the prearranged signal; he shoots the arrow and sends the lad after it. "And when the lad came to the place of the arrow which Jonathan had shot, Jonathan called after the lad and said, 'Is not the arrow beyond you?'" (20:37). This is the agreed upon sign that Saul's reaction was negative.

> And behold, I will send the lad, saying, "Go, find the arrows." If I say to the lad, "Look, the arrows are on this side of you, take them," then you are to come, for, as the Lord lives, it is safe for you and there is no danger. But if I say to the youth, "Look, the arrows are beyond you," then go; for the Lord has sent you away. (20:21–22)

But, despite the sign, David does not go away, and Jonathan remains in the field after he orders his lad to take the weapons back to the city.

> And Jonathan called after the lad, "Hurry, make haste, stay not." So Jonathan's lad gathered up the arrows, and came to his master. But the lad knew nothing; only Jonathan and

David knew the matter. And Jonathan gave his weapons to
his lad, and said to him, "Go and carry them to the city."
And as soon as the lad had gone, David rose from beside
the stone heap and fell on his face to the ground, and
bowed three times; and they kissed one another, and wept
with one another . . . Then Jonathan said to David, "Go in
peace, forasmuch as we have sworn both of us in the name
of the Lord, saying, 'The Lord shall be between me and
you, and between my descendants and your descendants,
for ever.'" And he rose and departed; and Jonathan went
into the city. (20:38–21:1)

The elaborate sign has fulfilled its purpose of communicating Saul's
reaction to the proffered excuse; when they meet, Jonathan has to
say nothing to David about Saul. The elaborate sign, for one of
several reasons, was superfluous from the start; both Jonathan and
David are convinced of Saul's intentions.

As a serious proposal, the sign was intended as a daytime event
performed before Saul himself, but since it is morning, he is not
there, and there is no need for secrecy. However, Jonathan still
carries through with the procedure until he can discharge the young
lad without arousing his suspicions, or Jonathan simply finds it
impossible not to play out the elaborate sign. On the other hand, the
sign was just show from its inception, a manifestation of Jonathan's
penchant for display and surreptitious signals. The expressed concern with Saul's reaction has been a cover for other issues and
desires; for Jonathan one such desire is the covenant with David.

Jonathan's call, "Hurry, make haste, stay not," is addressed
directly to the lad. For whatever reason, Jonathan wants to end the
arrow shooting exercise quickly, and he orders the lad to come back
and to go to the city. "The lad knew nothing" and why risk that he
might learn something? If the call is also meant for David, as
according to the arrangment in 20:22, David does not heed it.

The final scene of the chapter opens with David's (mock?)
ceremony: "[he] fell on his face to the ground, and bowed three
times." For the third and final time, Jonathan invokes the oath
between himself and David and between their descendants, "Go in
peace, forasmuch as we have sworn both of us in the name of the
Lord, saying, 'The Lord shall be between you and me, and between
my descendants and your descendants, for ever.'" With this parting
reminder, it can be said that Jonathan has made his point about his
desire for a covenant between himself and David, a covenant that

in some fashion should protect him and his descendants. The covenant is perhaps later renewed after Jonathan has come to Horesh to encourage David: "and the two of them made a covenant before the Lord" (23:18). Or the latter oath is a different agreement between the two, an agreement concerning Jonathan's being "second-in-command" to David. The text supports both and other readings.

Yet in no instance are we given any explicit information on what David thinks he is swearing to or on how he regards any oaths or covenants that he has made with Jonathan. We do get declarations from Jonathan, but there are only narrational notes that David did swear or make a covenant. David says nothing about the oaths; there are no statements by him which can be assessed and weighed. David's later treatment of Mephibosheth, Jonathan's son, in 2 Samuel 9 is too equivocal in its motivation—sincere concern or shrewd political move?—to regard it as proof that David felt bound by a covenant with Jonathan to maintain and protect his descendants. "And David said, 'Is there still any one left of the house of Saul, that I may show him kindness for Jonathan's sake?'" (2 Sam 9:1). David feels bound by his previous covenant with Jonathan; David does not feel bound by any earlier covenant, but will use the covenant with Jonathan as an opportunity to "keep an eye on" a remaining member of the house of Saul. Or . . . again, a continuum.

Although something can be asserted of what Jonathan had derived from the meeting with David in 1 Samuel 20, little or nothing can be said of what gain has come to David himself. Perhaps he now regards Jonathan as an effective ally, or even a spy, but the continuing narrative of 1 Samuel does not confirm this since David does not again come to Jonathan for help or information. Indeed, that David does not come may indicate his realization that Jonathan is not an effective spy; Jonathan is too self-involved or Saul is simply too angry at him and distrustful of him.

The speculation about David and Jonathan, particularly about Jonathan in his relationships with David and Saul, could continue, but a portrayal of Jonathan remains indeterminate. After his encouragement of David at Horesh, the narrative speaks one more time of Jonathan:

> Now the Philistines fought against Israel; and the men of Israel fled before the Philistines, and fell slain on Mount Gilboa. And the Philistines overtook Saul and his sons; and the Philistines slew Jonathan and Abinadab and Malchishua, the sons of Saul . . . On the morrow, when the Philistines came to

strip the slain, they found Saul and his three sons fallen on
Mount Gilboa. (1 Sam 31:1–8)

1 Samuel 21:2–10:
David and Ahimelech: A Deception

After departing from Jonathan, David goes to the sanctuary at
Nob where he meets with the priest Ahimelech; the majority of
1 Samuel 21–22 is concerned with the meeting and its aftermath
which concludes with the violent destruction of the house of Ahimelech. The two chapters offer us clarity because they employ several
modes of repetition and the repetition should elucidate the narrative itself and perhaps some of the preceding material. The main
events at Nob, which are narrated in 21:2–10 (Engl. 21:1–9), are
referred to in retrospect by the three characters who were there,
David, Ahimelech, and Doeg the Edomite (22:9–23). There is a
reference to David's defeat of Goliath and to the song that was sung
to David and Saul as they returned from the battle front. David's
flight to the Philistines in Gath, Goliath's city, is surprising, but does
raise the possibility that the Philistines may provide clarification of
their view of David and of the duel with Goliath.

Ahimelech, the priest of Nob, is the third person David encounters in his flight from Saul. The story is reminiscent of Samuel's trip
to Bethlehem to anoint David (1 Sam 16:1–13). Both incidents
involve deception, trembling at meeting the lone figure, consecra-
tion (Heb.: *qdš*), and sacrificial food. 1 Samuel 16 is followed by the
David and Goliath story, 1 Sam 21:2–10 alludes back to it. Just as
1 Samuel 17 did not clarify the questions left by 1 Samuel 16,
1 Samuel 21–22 do not resolve the problems left by 1 Samuel 17,
20, or the earlier parts of 1 Samuel 21–22. The entire chain of
events which revolves around Ahimelech involves references and
allusions to the past, but they lack the necessary specificity or trustworthiness to reconstruct a narrative of the past from them.

"Then came David to Nob to Ahimelech the priest; and Ahimelech came to meet David trembling, and said to him, 'Why are you
alone, and no one with you?'" (21:2). The trembling may be behavior
that is appropriate in the presence of authority as the elders of
Bethlehem tremble at Samuel's approach (16:4; see Smith, 197). Or
Ahimelech may suspect that David is in flight because he is alone and
therefore is in some danger (McCarter, 349). Ahimelech's questions

presume earlier contact between David and Ahimelech when the former was accompanied by other men; later Ahimelech tells Saul that David has come to Nob previously (22:14–15). David's response to Ahimelech is a lie. He tells him that Saul has sent him on a secret mission, that he is to meet his other men soon, and that he left with such urgency that he brought no food or weapons with him. Although David's alibi is false, his need for food and weapons is real. The narrative can, in this regard, be broken into two parts, obtaining the bread and the sword of Goliath, with the break marked by vs. 8, the notice of Doeg's presence at Nob.

In accord with his story and his need, David asks first for bread. "Now then, what have you at hand? Give me five loaves of bread, or whatever is here" (21:3). The detail of "five loaves" is intriguing and will be followed in another reading of the David story. However, Ahimelech has no ordinary bread, only holy bread, the bread of the Presence, which he can give to David provided the men have had no sexual contact with women. This must have been surprising to David, but he responds directly to the restriction with a forceful assurance that the men are holy, consecrated. David continues his lie; as a "man prudent in speech" he is not caught in the lie. The interpretation corresponds with one of the explications proposed for David's conversation with Jonathan in the preceding narrative, i.e., David has a purpose in mind and says whatever the immediate situation requires him to say to attain his desire.

Ahimelech gives him the holy bread, "for there was no bread there but the bread of the Presence, which is removed from before the Lord, to be replaced by hot bread on the day it is taken away" (21:7). This is another interesting detail. Is it stressing that "this sacred bread is appropriate for the chosen king" (Ackroyd, 171)? Is it, and perhaps including the following episode of David taking Goliath's sword from the sanctuary "from behind the ephod," emphasizing that David recognizes neither secular nor sacred constraints? Could there also be a comment on Ahimelech's competence and his (im)proper maintenance of the sanctuary?

The narrative notes that "a certain man of the servants of Saul was there that day, detained before the Lord; his name was Doeg the Edomite, the chief of Saul's herdsmen" (21:8). The significance of "being detained before the Lord" is not apparent; there is a play on David's foregoing statement that "women have been kept [Heb.: detained] from us" (21:6). "The chief of Saul's shepherds": this is an ironic allusion to David as shepherd (see 16:11 and 17:15), but Doeg will be no David. Later David tells Abiathar that he himself saw Doeg at the sanctuary (22:22); there is little reason to doubt the declaration.

David then makes what is probably an even more urgent request of Ahimelech, "Have you not here a spear or a sword at hand?" (21:9). Ahimelech presents him with "the sword of Goliath the Philistine whom you killed in the valley of Elah" (21:10). Did Ahimelech see the battle or only hear of it? His statement is tantalizing, but says nothing more of the event or its aftermath. The sword is "behind the ephod"; the phrase foreshadows Abiathar's escape to David "with an ephod in his hand" (22:20 and 23:6). David accepts the sword from Ahimelech, and the theme of violence is thereby reintroduced into the narrative and associated with David. It is not by chance that bloody violence will soon transpire. Doeg massacres the priests of Nob and the entire city (22:18–19), and then David makes "a great slaughter" (23:5).

1 Samuel 22:11–16:
David and Achish: A Second Deception

"And David rose and fled that day from Saul, and went to Achish the king of Gath" (21:11 [Engl. 21:10]). David encounters the fourth person in his flight. Why does David go to Gath? Is this just the next stage in his headlong flight from Saul? Does David leave Nob and its vicinity because he knows that Doeg will tell Saul that he saw him there? Or does David have some specific, although unexpressed, reason for going to Gath? Does he go to the Philistines feeling certain that Saul will not and cannot pursue him there? At the news of David's second escape to the Philistines in Gath, Saul definitively ends his pursuit of David; "when it was told Saul that David had fled to Gath, he sought for him no more" (1 Sam 27:4). The first trip to Gath does not have that effect because David soon has to leave and return to Judah.

Achish's servants see David upon his arrival in Gath and ask Achish, "Is not this David the king of the land?" (21:12). The "question" foreshadows David's later status, but in its context it is a mistake, an overevaluation. The servants continue,

> Did they not sing to one another of him in dances,
>   'Saul has slain his thousands,
>   and David his ten thousands'? (21:12)

This is the couplet that the women of Israel sang to David and Saul as "he returned from slaying the Philistine," Goliath of Gath

(18:6–7). At that time Saul reacted to the song with anger, displeasure, and jealousy; this time David reacts with fear. "And David took these words to heart, and was much afraid of Achish the king of Gath" (21:13). David relies on deception and pretends to be mad; he "made marks on the door of the gate, and let his spittle run down his beard" (21:14). Achish is gulled by the pretense. "Do I lack madmen, that you have brought this fellow to play the madman in my presence? Shall this fellow come into my house?" (21:16). The closing "question" is an ironic forecast of David's return to Achish when he will again be gulled by David. At that time the couplet is quoted for the third and final time by the Philistine commanders; their reaction to the song is distrust of David, and he is again dismissed (1 Samuel 29).

David's second flight to Achish of Gath to escape Saul follows readily upon his experience in the first visit there. The Philistines are no threat to David since they, particularly Achish, are easily tricked. They overestimate his position in Israel and, for some reason, do not connect David with the slaughter of hundreds of their own, including the Gittite warrior Goliath. Indeed, David may have Goliath's sword with him as a visible reminder. Or is this evidence that Elhanan, not David, killed Goliath?

1 Samuel 22:6–19: The Massacre of Nob

For the time being, I skip the two incidents at Adullam and Moab in 1 Sam 22:1–5 to go to the scene at Gibeah of Benjamin. "Saul was sitting at Gibeah, under the tamarisk tree on the height, with his spear in his hand, and all his servants were standing about him" (22:6). Saul upbraids his servants for not informing him of the pact between David and his son Jonathan. "No one discloses to me when my son makes a league with the son of Jesse, none of you is sorry for me or discloses to me that my son has stirred up my servant against me, to lie in wait, as at this day" (22:8). Doeg the Edomite is present at the Gibeah court. He has nothing to report about David and Jonathan, but he can inform Saul that "I saw the son of Jesse coming to Nob, to Ahimelech the son of Ahitub, and he inquired of the Lord for him, and gave him provisions, and gave him the sword of Goliath the Philistine" (22:9–10). The details of the statement are striking, particularly as they relate to the preceding narrative of David at Nob.

Doeg refers to Ahimelech as "the son of Ahitub." The genealogical information was not presented in the foregoing story when it

would have seemed most appropriate. However, there is another
example of such a delay in providing information in the very next
chapter. It is only after the narration of Abiathar's flight to David
and of David's consulting the Lord through him that it is reported
"when Abiathar . . . fled to David . . . he came down with an
ephod in his hand" (23:6). The technique of delayed information is
not restricted to these passages; it has been analyzed further by
Weiss.

Ahimelech is called the "son of Ahitub" three more times in
1 Samuel 22; twice by Saul in verses 11 and 12 and once by the
narration itself in vs. 20. Apparently Ahitub is the son of Phinehas,
the son of Eli, and therefore Ahimelech is a member of the doomed
house of Eli (see 1 Sam 14:3 and 1 Kgs 2:27). This is fitting in light
of the events that are soon to transpire.

"He inquired of the Lord for him." The action is not reported
in the narrative in 21:2–7, but will be confirmed soon by Ahimelech
himself. "And gave him provisions." In the ensuing dialogue in
1 Samuel 22, no one—Doeg, Saul, or Ahimelech—will refer to the
fact that the "provisions" were holy bread, the bread of the Presence. If their failure to mention it indicates that taking the holy
bread was not a serious transgression of sacral law, then why is it so
central in the preceding narrative? Or, vice versa, if it was so
important there, why is it glossed over here? Could it be that Doeg
did not realize what the provisions actually were, and Ahimelech is
not going to incriminate himself further with Saul by mentioning
the holy bread? The "omission" of this portion of the narrative in
21:2–7 is "balanced" by the "addition" of the charge that Ahimelech
inquired of the Lord for David which is not part of the previous
narrative. Finally, "and gave him the sword of Goliath the
Philistine." This would seem to be a serious charge, yet Saul makes
little of it. "Why have you conspired against me, you and the son of
Jesse, in that you have given him *bread and a sword*, and have
inquired of God for him?" (22:13).

Saul summons Ahimelech, "and all his father's house, the priests
who were at Nob," to Gibeah and charges him with conspiring
against him, "you and the son of Jesse" (22:11–13). Just before this,
Saul had charged the Benjaminites with conspiring against him, but
not of conspiring with "the son of Jesse." Saul cites his evidence of
Ahimelech's conspiracy—bread, sword, and inquiry of God—and
the results of the conspiracy: "so that he has risen against me, to lie
in wait, as at this day" (21:13). This is almost identical to his prior

charge against the Benjaminites in 22:8. Ahimelech answers this final part of Saul's charge by affirming that David is too faithful and too close to the king to ever turn against him in rebellion.

Ahimelech then rejects Saul's accusation that he himself did anything wrong in consulting the Lord on David's behalf. The Hebrew text of his reply is susceptible of at least two different translations; neither denies that Ahimelech did consult the Lord and both can refer to the fact that Ahimelech has done this before for David.

> Is today the first time that I have inquired of God for him? No! (*RSV*)

> Have I on this occasion done something profane in consulting God on his behalf? God forbid! (*NEB*) (22:15)

Previously Doeg the Edomite had said nothing of having seen David at Nob until Saul rebuked his servants; perhaps he originally thought that there was nothing amiss with David's presence at the sanctuary. Ahimelech closes his defense with a general request that the king not accuse him or his family of anything, "for your servant has known nothing of all this, much or little" (21:15). Whatever Ahimelech did for David, he did it in ignorance of any break or of any hostility between David and Saul.

Saul pronounces judgment, "You shall surely die, Ahimelech, you and all your father's house" (22:16). Whether or not Saul has accepted Ahimelech's defense, his sentence means death for Ahimelech and his entire family. This raises the distinct possibility that Saul is not interested in punishing a particular act of treason, but in eradicating a whole group of potential enemies and also in making an example of them for the Benjaminites gathered there at Gibeah. The interpretation is supported by Saul's initial summons, not just of Ahimelech, but of all his family. Further, when Saul orders his guard to kill all of them, it is "because their hand also is with David, and they knew that he fled, and did not disclose it to me" (21:17). He had previously accused the Benjamanites of not informing him of the league between his son and David. At the same time, Saul's stated reason renders Ahimelech's defense superfluous since now it does not matter what Ahimelech did or what he knew, he told Saul nothing of David. Saul defines such silence as treason, in the cases of both Ahimelech and the Benjaminites. The condemnation is to be contrasted with the praise that Saul later bestows on the Ziphites for telling him of David's whereabouts: "May you be blessed by the Lord; for you have had compassion on me" (23:21).

They evidently derived the proper conclusion from the example of the house of Ahimelech.

If Ahimelech did inquire of the Lord for David, why is it omitted from the narrative in 21:2–7? I have already noted two other examples of the delayed presentation of information in 1 Samuel 22 and 23. Such an omission in 1 Samuel 21 serves then to emphasize the act of inquiring of the Lord once it is mentioned by Doeg and repeated by Saul and Ahimelech. "Inquiry of the Lord" recalls Saul's previous aborted or unsuccessful attempts to consult the Lord during the battle with the Philistines (14:18–19, 36–37) and foreshadows his final, futile attempt to inquire of the Lord in 1 Samuel 28 which leads him to call up Samuel from the dead (28:6, 15). It also points to David's successful consultations of the Lord at Keilah (1 Sam 23:1–12), at Ziklag (1 Sam 30:7–8), and when he becomes king of Judah (2 Sam 2:1–4).

On the other hand, perhaps the charge was fabricated by Doeg to make the accusation against David (and against Ahimelech?) as damaging as possible. Ahimelech does not deny the charge because he sees nothing wrong with the action even though he had not actually consulted the Lord for David. Further, his defense is an assertion of his full innocence in anything that he has done, not a denial that he has done something.

> But the servants of the king would not put forth their hand to fall upon the priests of the Lord. Then the king said to Doeg, "You turn and fall upon the priests." And Doeg the Edomite turned and fell upon the priests, and he killed on that day eighty-five persons who wore the linen ephod. And Nob, the city of the priests, he put to the sword; both men and women, children and sucklings, oxen, asses and sheep, he put to the sword. (22:17–19)

Through the hand of a foreigner Saul perpetrates upon Israelites what he himself failed to perpetrate upon foreigners, the Amalekites, Israel's arch-enemy; "but Saul and the people spared Agag, and the best of the sheep and of the oxen and of the fatlings, and the lambs . . ." (1 Sam 15:9).

1 Samuel 22:20–23: A Sole Survivor

> But one of the sons of Ahimelech the son of Ahitub, named Abiathar, escaped and fled after David. And Abiathar told

> David that Saul had killed the priests of the Lord.
> (22:20–21)

The theme of the sole survivor was encountered above, and it is here again associated with David (above, 95). David responds to Abiathar's statement, "I knew on that day, when Doeg the Edomite was there, that he would surely tell Saul" (22:22). I previously noted that this knowledge of David's is a possible motivation for his flight to Achish of Gath. "I have occasioned the death of all the persons of your father's house" (22:22). The violence of Doeg, which he carried out with "the sword," attaches itself to David. In the context, this is a statement of fact on David's part, but not necessarily an admission of guilt, since David says no more of it nor does he bewail the catastrophe. The incident closes with David's command to Abiathar, "Stay with me, fear not, for he that seeks my life seeks your life; with me you shall be in safekeeping" (22:23). (Unpacking of the assurance and its "logic" will have to await a future reading.) Whatever David's opinion is of his involvement in the slaughter of Abiathar's family, the episode ends with Abiathar bound to David for his protection.

David's Support Groups

The group of people that David meets in his flight from Saul, beginning with Samuel in 19:19–24, are frequently interpreted, in various ways and to different degrees, as pointing to support for David that comes from all parts and levels of society. McCarter's comment on 19:19–24 is fairly thorough and representative of the approach:

> Once he is safely out of Gibeah, David makes his way to the prophetic encampments near Ramah where he confers with Samuel. This is the first in a series of interviews between David and various individuals who assist his escape, viz. Samuel, Jonathan, and Ahimelech of Nob, to each of whom he goes in turn. All of them are important people—Ahimelech and Jonathan may be said to represent "church and state" to some extent—so that their support of the fugitive hero is especially significant. A new theme, for which we were prepared by Michal's part in the preceding incident, is introduced here: David is protected from Saul by the leading citizens of Saul's kingdom. (32:9–30)

My close reading of the concerned texts demonstrates that David's protection from Saul can be a theme in them, but not always a certain and definite theme and never the only theme, the "meaning" of the series of meetings. Ahimelech certainly helps David with the provision of bread and a sword, but the narrative does not unequivocally state that either Samuel or Jonathan actually aided David in his escape. This is not to say that they did not; it is not to decide for an interpretation that is the opposite of McCarter's. It is a "line" of interpretation composed of indeterminate "points."

Nevertheless the style of explication exemplified by McCarter is interesting and can be expanded with profit. As with much of the above reading, I propose a continuum and lay out two poles on it. The first pole is that of McCarter and others. The narrative in 1 Sam 19:9–22:23 is concerned with a group of people who, with one exception, aid David in his flight from Saul: Michal, Samuel, Jonathan, Ahimelech, a band of outlaws (22:1–2), the king of Moab, the prophet Gad, and Abiathar the priest. David is supported by representatives of various parts of "church and state," both high and low classes. The one person from whom he does not receive any help is Achish, the king of Gath. This is appropriate since Israelites, not foreigners, are to help David escape and eventually to become king himself.

The other pole: Michal does help David escape by informing him of Saul's attempt on his life and by deceiving Saul's messengers to give David time to get away (19:11–17). Samuel turns out to be of little or no use; Saul may prophesy in his presence, but he does not then yield in his murderous pursuit of David. Jonathan also proves to be of no help for one or more of a variety of reasons. Ahimelech can give David succor in his immediate flight; but it is not long term. David must flee from Nob to Gath; he has to leave his own land and go to the Philistines for relief. This indicates that Ahimelech's help is of limited value. Nor do the Philistines provide support; indeed, they themselves present a danger to David. Ironically, the Philistines do, at one point, help David to escape.

> David was making haste to get away from Saul, as Saul and his men were closing in upon David and his men to capture them, when a messenger came to Saul, saying, "Make haste and come; for the Philistines have made a raid upon the land." So Saul returned from pursuing after David, and went against the Philistines; therefore that place was called the Rock of Escape. (23:26–28)

After fleeing from Achish of Gath, David returns to Judah to the cave at Adullam where "his brothers and all his father's house" join him (22:1).

> And every one who was in distress, and every one who was
> in debt, and every one who was discontented, gathered to
> him; and he became captain over them. And there were
> with him about four hundred men. (22:2)

If this is support, it is ironic. "Saul also went to his home at Gibeah,
and with him went men of valor whose hearts God had touched"
(10:26). "And when Saul saw any strong man, or any valiant man,
he attached him to himself" (14:52).

David's family, at least his parents, prove to be more of a hin-
drance than a help.

> And David went from there to Mizpeh of Moab; and he
> said to the king of Moab, "Pray let my father and my
> mother come out with you, till I know what God will do for
> me." And he left them with the king of Moab, and they
> stayed with him all the time that David was in the strong-
> hold. (22:3–4)

Nothing more is said in the narrative of David's parents or his
brothers. Soon David leaves "the stronghold" at the behest of a
prophet. "Then the prophet Gad said to David, 'Do not remain in
the stronghold; depart and go into the land of Judah'" (23:5). Does
this indicate that his parents accompany him when he returns to
Judah? What precisely is and where is "the stronghold"? Is it the
same "stronghold" as in 1 Sam 24:23 and in 2 Sam 5:7–17 and 23:14
(see above, 91–92)?

Has the prophet Gad helped David? No reason for his command
to David is given. Is David in some danger in Moab as he felt he was in
Gath? Gad's only other appearance is in 2 Samuel 24 where he brings
a message of judgment to David and presents him with a choice of
three punishments: famine, flight, or pestilence (2 Sam 24:11–14). "Or
will you flee three months before your foes while they pursue?" Gad
asks David. Future reading will have to develop the parallel further,
particularly in light of the unsettling effects of other incidents in
2 Samuel 21–24 on the reading of the David story.

Finally, Abiathar, the sole surviving priest of Nob, comes to
David with an ephod. Abiathar will be with David for the rest of
David's life and will be of some help, but he is a member of the
doomed house of Eli. The impact of the man of God's speech in
1 Sam 2:27–36 on a reading of the David story and of the continuing narrative in the books of Kings will have to be assessed in other
readings. Abiathar is eventually banished by Solomon to his estate

of Anathoth; "So Solomon expelled Abiathar from being priest to the Lord, thus fulfilling the word of the Lord which he had spoken concerning the house of Eli in Shiloh" (1 Kgs 2:27). Solomon expels him, but throughout his life David is associated with the curse on the house of Eli through Abiathar his priest.

The Reading Stops

This brings my reading of the David story to a close. I stop with 1 Samuel 22 since 1 Samuel 23 introduces issues that would carry us far beyond the scope of these readings. Foremost is "inquiry of God" which I discussed in the reading of 1 Samuel 21–22, but which I did not pursue in length. Related topics are priests, prophets, the role of God, etc. These are reserved for future readings.

NOTES

/1/   Above (38) I noted the disconcerting effect of 2 Sam 21:8 which notes that Michal had five children.

/2/   Consult Miscall (1978) for discussion of the Joseph story. In "The Difficulty of Ruling Well," Gros Louis has analyzed the David story in 1–2 Samuel as revolving around David the effective public ruler who is brought down by his failure to control his private desires and his own family, particularly his sons.

/3/   I propose "In the days of Saul, the man was an elder and distinguished among men" as a rendering of the Hebrew text without emendation.

/4/   Depending on the context, I vary my translation of *'îš yiśrā'ēl* and *'am yiśrā'ēl* between "men/people of Israel" and "army of Israel."

/5/   For discussion of the problematic status of "questions," see P. de Man, *Allegories of Reading*, pp. 3–19.

/6/   I note the necessity for further analysis of the references to "youth" and "young man" in these stories, e.g., 1 Sam 14:1–15; 17:32–58; 20:35–41; 21:3–6 (Engl. 21:2–5).

/7/   McCarter "solves" the problem of 1 Sam 17:50–51 by assigning each verse to independent accounts that were combined much later (284–309). He translates vs. 51, "David ran up and stood beside him. He took his sword and dispatched him, cutting off his head" (285). McCarter notes that the Hebrew verb he translated "to dispatch" occurs with this sense in Judg 9:54; 1 Sam 14:13; 2 Sam 1:9, 10, 16. Others, e.g., Hertzberg, agree with this translation, but do not so definitively separate the two verses. Hertzberg opines that "we are probably to understand that Goliath falls down stunned and is only slain by the blow from David's sword." He continues,

> The interposed v. 50, referring to v. 47, underlines the fact
> that the victory was not won with ordinary weapons. Here
> we have the climax of the theological standpoint which has
> been adopted here. We need therefore see no contradiction
> to the surrounding sentences in the statement of v. 50. . . .
> What is stressed here . . . was that God had done his saving
> work without there having been a sword in the hand of his
> chosen instrument. (153)

Yet, Hertzberg himself opened the discussion by asserting that "Goliath
falls down stunned and is only slain by the blow from David's sword."

/8/   I will frequently cite McCarter's translation and will note the
page number in his commentary.

/9/   Parallels between David and Joseph are not new and have been
noted and developed by others, e.g., Stoebe and Brueggemann.

/10/   Alter's discovery of the "type-scene" stems from his reading of
Culley's *Studies in the Structure of Hebrew Narrative.* Culley, however, is
concerned to find evidence of oral narration in repeated stories, i.e., to use
Alter's phrase he is searching for "a single *ur*-story." Therefore, Culley
focuses on the episodes independent of their context with the intent of
demonstrating that the same plot elements occur even though other elements and characters are different.

Alter argues, and I would concur, that Culley misses the point, that he
has "made a discovery without even dimly realizing it." The episodes do
not reveal "a scrambling by oral transmission," but "the lineaments of a
purposefully deployed literary convention." Culley misses this because his
approach isolates the episodes from their literary context and regards the
differences, the specifics of each episode, as secondary. He cannot conduct
the sort of literary analysis that Alter or I do (Alter, 358; his italics).

/11/   McCarter argues for a change in the text and translates, "But
indeed, as Yahweh lives and as you yourself live, he has sworn a pact
between me and Death" (322 and explanatory note on 335).

/12/   1 Sam 20:25 is generally emended with the Greek to something
like "Jonathan sat opposite" (McCarter, 333, and *RSV*) or "Jonathan was in
front of him" (Ackroyd, 167). Keil and Delitzsch cannot emend the text,
therefore they supplement it:

> The difficult passage, "*And Jonathan rose up,*" etc., can
> hardly be understood in any other way than as signifying
> that, when Abner entered, Jonathan rose from his seat by
> the side of Saul, and gave up the place to Abner, in which
> case all that is wanting is an account of the place to which
> Jonathan moved. (212; their italics)

POSTSCRIPT

The postscript is writing "after-the-written." It is not a conclusion, a "closing" or "shutting" of what has been written. It is an introduction, a leading back into what has already been written and forward into what has yet to be written. The postscript is not an exhaustive presentation of or argument in defense of my readings and mode of reading. The readings themselves are the heart of the work. Another work can, and perhaps will, present the issues of this postscript in fuller form. My goal now is to set my mode of reading within the context of contemporary literary criticism and to point to some future avenues of research beyond the specific pointers given in the work. The presentation is personal and limited; I am not attempting to explicate or defend certain trends in contemporary literary criticism.

The readings in the book represent a definite break with the standard historical-critical modes of reading OT narrative and, to a large extent, with newer literary approaches to the biblical material such as structuralism and New Criticism. As asserted in the Introduction and throughout the book, I do not make an attempt to establish "the meaning" of the text if such establishment means "controlling" or "stopping" the text by imposing some framework or limits on it that endeavour to overcome the specific text and its ever increasing parallels. This applies regardless of whether that meaning is defined as religious, historical, social, theological, etc. Whether I do or can avoid such control is a matter for future concern; at present, just the attempt to avoid it takes me far from contemporary biblical criticism.

My focus has been on the "textuality" of the text, the text as a written and material entity with its own status, whether decidable or not, and its own modes of working. Because of the restriction of my reading to selected passages and their parallels plus some relevant commentaries, I have given little attention to the closely related, if not synonymous, notion of "intertextuality," i.e., a given text exists because of its differences from and relations to the network(s) of other texts. Again, as so frequently in the book, this is a topic for future consideration.

I have sought not to subordinate the text to something else, to something "outside" it, particularly something that precedes it and can therefore control it by having author-ity over it. Thus, the point of my discussion of the biblical commentaries on Genesis and 1 Samuel is not a presentation and critique of the approach of one commentary or of the overall historical-critical approach. The point is to demonstrate some of the major ways in which they seek to control and stop the text by reducing it to, or replacing it with, another text, variously called "redactor's purpose," "author's intention," "historical meaning," "theological teaching," etc. This "other text" is then given author-ity over the primary text. They establish the meaning, purpose, "truth," or such, of a text only by leaving something out, by missing or ignoring something; I focus on their omission, their suppression, of so many of the troublesome details, gaps, repetitions, contradictions, etc., pertaining to the passage(s) under consideration. Future study will have to shift its attention to a more detailed and exhaustive reading of the commentaries and ask of them again, "What does such 'truth' (or any 'truth') leave out?" and be prepared for quite different answers from those that I have given here. Finally, I or another can turn and ask the present work, "What has it left out? What residue or remainder does it not account for?" (Felman, 117).

Some of the terminology that I have employed, e.g., "undecidable" and "indeterminate," plus the tenor of the readings and some of the bibliography cited indicate that the general setting within contemporary literary criticism for my work is the area referred to as deconstruction and sometimes post-structuralism. I do not present my work as deconstructive readings of the OT text. They are close and sustained readings of selected texts, and the mode of reading is informed by a variety of critical approaches, including structuralism and deconstruction.

The readings are frequently, if not always, "decidedly undecidable" and seem to leave no room for a determinate reading, e.g., of David. Yes and no. For my work, I at present see no way that I would decide for a specific portrayal of David, even if it is rich and open-ended. My work on the OT will continue to stress its indeterminateness and will attempt to demonstrate the latter in even more radical and far-reaching senses. On the other hand, others of

whatever critical persuasion—historical-critical, structuralist, phe-
nomenological, hermeneutical, etc.—can argue, and argue forcefully, for such determinate readings, but this would not prevent a
counter-argument that they have so determined the reading only by
suppressing parts of the text and by adding other elements to it.
Nor would this prevent their counter-argument, etc.

In regard to deconstructive critics, the main influences on
myself have been Jacques Derrida, Paul de Man, J. Hillis Miller,
and Geoffrey H. Hartman. (I note that Hartman can be considered
a deconstructive critic only in a very broad sense of the phrase.)
Reading of their works is a far better and more thorough introduction to deconstruction than any I could provide in this limited
space. Their works that I have included in my bibliography are
selected, but are the ones that I have read and consulted most frequently. Hartman's *Criticism in The Wilderness* is an excellent
treatment of many of the issues and problems of deconstruction.
Many literary journals carry articles concerning deconstructive criticism. Some, e.g., *Diacritics*, *Glyph*, and *Yale French Studies*, devote
a large amount of their space to the subject.

The work of critics such as Wolfgang Iser, Stanley Fish, and
Harold Bloom could also be relevant to my project. I have not yet
read their work extensively and intensively enough to assess their
relevance and to locate areas of agreement and disagreement with
what I am attempting to do. However, in a recent review of Iser's
The Act of Reading, Fish claims that Iser's work and theory, which
focuses on how a reader "fills in" the indeterminate parts of a work,
ultimately fails because it depends finally on the firm distinction
between the determinate and the indeterminate, i.e., "between
what is already given and what must be brought into being by
interpretive activity" (6).

Fish, in deconstructive fashion, challenges the distinction itself:
"there is no distinction between what the text gives and what the
reader supplies" (7). For Fish, the distinction is not independent,
but is a part of a specific interpretive strategy. I find the critique
forceful and troubling since it bears upon my approach which
incorporates a similar distinction, e.g., the "there, but not here"
effect. For the future, I will need to take the critique into account
and to assess its impact on my interpretive strategy. I note now that
I would agree with Fish. (I also note the similar argument of
Richard Rorty in his recent and influential *Philosophy and the
Mirror of Nature*.)

For the present, I note that my concern with and my strong resistance to essentialist interpretations and reductions of the biblical text are a mark of much deconstructive criticism. The concern and resistance have a corollary in the deconstructive goal of demonstrating that a text has already undermined itself, that its status is already undecidable because of itself and not because of some error in logic, evidence, argument, etc. Deconstructive criticism is not primarily concerned with unearthing the questionable presuppositions, hidden contradictions, etc., within a text; to do this would be to suggest that another work could avoid all of its presuppositions, contradictions, etc., and thereby arrive at fullness and truth. Deconstruction regards a written work as the product of writing and language, and the latter are held to be equivocal, slippery, open, changing, etc. Writing and language do not produce full and essential meanings because of their own nature and not because of some error in their use. Another book may avoid the problematic presuppositions and the contradictions of the preceding work, but it cannot avoid the problematics of writing and language. From another perspective, deconstructive criticism can be said to be ferreting out the places where a text "slips," where its authority is undermined, simply because it is a written text.

My readings have sought to demonstrate how the biblical text undermines itself, puts its own status and authority into question. This brings me to the border of my readings, but the border is also the frontier for my future work which I have frequently pointed to in the course of the book. There remains one general area that I wish to indicate.

I have only hinted at the general concept of narrative and narrativity. Given the readings I have done and am doing, how can I best describe OT narrative? What am I to make of the constant repetitions, "inconsistencies" and "contradictions" of the text? I have not had always to "ferret out" places where the OT text slips, where it undermines itself, since the "inconsistencies" and "contradictions" are generally rather obvious. What is to be made of the ease with which one can demonstrate problematics of OT narrative?

In my research, I have found that all the notions of narrative and the related issues—plot, character, theme, etc.—which are derived from some part of Western literature are of limited value in the analysis of biblical narrative. For example, New Critical and structuralist theories and readings of narrative and its various aspects certainly give me added insight into the biblical text. I come away knowing more of the text and its workings, but also knowing that the text has escaped the theory and the readings, that parts of it are not accounted for, and that therefore the theory is flawed, perhaps beyond repair. "Perhaps beyond repair": I am not sure that it is a matter of adjusting the theory of narrative in view of the biblical text; it may, on the other hand, be a matter of putting into question the very notions of narrative and narrativity, of looking into their status. Thus, I prefer the phrase "biblical text" to "biblical narrative." I am drawn to deconstructive criticism since I find many of the critics raising similar problems and writing of radical questioning and displacement of "fundamental concepts," including "fundamental" and "concept," and not just of adjusting them to fit a new situation. Deconstructive criticism allows me to think the OT as other than Western literature.

BIBLIOGRAPHY

Ackroyd, Peter
1971   *1 Samuel* (*The Cambridge Bible Commentary*). Cambridge: Cambridge University Press.

Alter, Robert
1975   "A Literary Approach to the Bible." *Commentary* 60:70–77.
1976   "Biblical Narrative." *Commentary* 61:61–67
1978a   "Biblical Type-Scenes and the Uses of Convention." *Critical Inquiry* 5:355–68.
1978b   "Character in the Bible." *Commentary* 66: 58–65.

Barthes, Roland
1968   "L'effet de réel." *Communications* 11:84–89.
1974   "The Struggle with the Angel: Textual Analysis of Genesis 32:23–33." Pp. 21–33 in *Structural Analysis and Biblical Exegesis*. By R. Barthes, *et. al.* (Pittsburgh Theological Monograph Series, 3). Pittsburgh: Pickwick.

Brueggemann, Walter
1972   "Life and Death in Tenth Century Israel." *JAAR* 40:96–109.

Cassuto, Umberto
1964   *A Commentary on the Book of Genesis.* Jerusalem: Magnes.

Clines, David J. A.
1979   "The Significance of the 'Sons of God' Episode (Genesis 6:1–4) in the Context of the

'Primeval History' (Genesis 1–11)." *JSOT* 13:33–46.

Culley, Robert C.
1976   *Studies in the Structure of Hebrew Narrative*. Philadelphia: Fortress.

De Man, Paul
1978   "The Epistemology of Metaphor." *Critical Inquiry* 5:13–30.

1979a   *Allegories of Reading*. New Haven: Yale.

1979b   "Shelley Disfigured." Pp. 39–73 in *Deconstruction and Criticism*. Eds. H. Bloom, *et. al*. New York: Seabury.

Derrida, Jacques
1976   *Of Grammatology*. Baltimore: Johns Hopkins.

1977a   "Signature Event Context." *Glyph* 1:172–97.

1977b   "Limited Inc." *Glyph* 2:162–254.

Felman, Shoshana
1977   "Turning the Screw of Interpretation." *Yale French Studies* 55/56:94–207.

Fish, Stanley
1981   "Why No One's Afraid of Wolfgang Iser." *Diacritics* 11:2–13.

Frei, Hans W.
1974   *The Eclipse of Biblical Narrative*. New Haven: Yale.

Genette, Gerard
1972   *Figures III*. Paris: Seuil.

Gros Louis, Kenneth R. R.
1977   "The Difficulty of Ruling Well: King David of Israel." *Semeia* 8:15–33.

Gunkel, Herrmann
1910   *Genesis*, 3rd ed. (HKAT 1/1). Göttingen: Vandenhoeck & Ruprecht. (Reissued unchanged in subsequent editions.)

Hartman, Geoffrey H.
1980   *Criticism In The Wilderness*. New Haven: Yale.

Hertzberg, Hans W.
    1964   *I & II Samuel: A Commentary*. Philadel-
                     phia: Westminster.

Iser, Wolfgang
    1979   *The Act of Reading: A Theory of Aesthetic
                     Response*. Baltimore: Johns Hopkins.

Jacob, B.
    1974   *Genesis: The First Book of The Bible*. New
                     York: KTAV.

Jobling, David
    1978   *The Sense of Biblical Narrative*. Sheffield:
                     JSOT Supplement Series, 7.

Keil, C. F. and Delitzsch, F.
    1971   *Commentary on the Old Testament in Ten
                     Volumes*. Vol. 1: The First Book of Moses
                     (Genesis); Vol. 5: The Books of Samuel.
                     Grand Rapids: Eerdmans.

Knierem, Rolf
    1968   "The Messianic Concept in the First Book of
                     Samuel." Pp. 20–51 in *Jesus and The Histo-
                     rian*. Ed. F. T. Trotter. Philadelphia: West-
                     minster.

Koch, Klaus
    1967   *The Growth of The Biblical Tradition*. New
                     York: Scribner.

Leitch, V. B.
    1980   "The Lateral Dance: The Deconstructive
                     Criticism of J. Hillis Miller." *Critical Inquiry*
                     6:593–607.

McCarter, P. Kyle, Jr.
    1980   *1 Samuel (The Anchor Bible*, 8). Garden
                     City, NY: Doubleday.

Miller, J. Hillis
    1978   "Ariadne's Thread: Repetition and the Narra-
                     tive Line." Pp. 148–66 in *Interpretations of
                     Narrative*. Eds. M. J. Valdes and O. J. Miller.
                     Toronto: University of Toronto Press.
    1979   "The Critic as Host." Pp. 217–53 in *Decon-

struction and Criticism. Eds. H. Bloom, *et. al.* New York: Seabury.

1980   "Theory and Practice: Response to Vincent Leitch." *Critical Inquiry* 6:609–14.

Miscall, Peter D.
1978   "The Jacob and Joseph Stories as Analogies." *JSOT* 6:28–40.

1979   "Literary Unity in Old Testament Narrative." *Semeia* 15:27–44

Nietzsche, Friedrich
1968   *The Will to Power.* Trans. W. Kaufmann and R. J. Hollingdale. New York: Random House, Vintage Books.

Petersen, David L.
1979   "Genesis 6:1–4, Yahweh and the Organization of the Cosmos." *JSOT* 13:47–64.

Plaut, W. Gunther
1974   *Genesis (The Torah: A Modern Commentary,* 1). New York: Union of American Hebrew Congregations.

Polzin, Robert
1975   "'The Ancestress of Israel in Danger' in Danger." *Semeia* 3:81–98.

Rad, Gerhard von
1961   *Genesis: A Commentary.* Philadelphia: Westminister

Rorty, Richard
1979   *Philosophy and the Mirror of Nature.* Princeton: Princeton.

Rose, Ashley S.
1974   "The 'Principles' of Divine Election. Wisdom in 1 Samuel, 16." Pp. 43–67 in *Rhetorical Criticism: Essays in Honor of James Muilenburg.* Eds. J. J. Jackson and M. Kessler. (Pittsburgh Theological Monograph Series, 1). Pittsburgh: Pickwick.

Sarna, Nahum M.
1966   *Understanding Genesis.* New York: McGraw-Hill.

Scholes, Robert
1974   *Structuralism in Literature.* New Haven: Yale.

Seybold, Donald A.
1974   "Paradox and Symmetry in the Joseph Narrative." Pp. 59–73 in *Literary Interpretations of Biblical Narratives.* Eds. K. R. R. Gros Louis, *et. al.* Nashville: Abingdon.

Skinner, John
1930   *Genesis (The International Critical Commentary,* 2nd ed.). Edinburgh: T & T. Clark.

Smith, Henry P.
1899   *The Books of Samuel (The International Critical Commentary).* Edinburgh: T. & T. Clark.

Speiser, E. A.
1964   *Genesis (The Anchor Bible,* 1). Garden City, NY: Doubleday.

Stoebe, H.-J.
1973   *Das erste Buch Samuelis (KZAT).* Gütersloh: Gerd Mohn.

Vawter, Bruce
1977   *On Genesis: A New Reading.* Garden City, NY: Doubleday.

Weiss, Meir
1965   "Weiteres über die Bauformen des Erzählens in der Bibel." *Biblica* 46:181–206.

Whitelam, Keith W.
1979   *The Just King: Monarchical Judicial Authority in Ancient Israel.* Sheffield: JSOT Supplement Series, 12.

Willis, John T.
1973   "The Function of Comprehensive Anticipatory Redactional Joints in I Samuel 16–18." *ZAW* 85:292–314.

Zuck, John E.
1976   "Tales of Wonder: Biblical Narrative, Myth, and Fairy Stories." *JAAR* 44:299–308.